The Fabian Society

The Fabian Society has played a central role for more than a century in the development of political ideas and public policy on the left of centre. Analysing the key challenges facing the UK and the rest of the industrialised world in a changing society and global economy, the Society's programme aims to explore the political ideas and the policy reforms which are defining progressive politics in the 21st century.

The Society is unique among think tanks in being a democratically-constituted membership organisation. It is affiliated to the Labour Party but is editorially and organisationally independent. Through its publications, seminars and conferences, the Society provides an arena for open-minded public debate.

Fabian Society
11 Dartmouth Street
London SW1H 9BN
www.fabian-society.org.uk

Series editor: Ellie Levenson

First published August 2003

ISBN 0 7163 3058 X

British Library Cataloguing in Publication data.
A catalogue record for this book is available from the British Library.

Printed by Crowes complete print, Norwich

A Better Choice of Choice

Quality of life, consumption and economic growth

Roger Levett
with Ian Christie, Michael Jacobs
and Riki Therivel

Contents

About the contributors

Roger Levett

Roger Levett is a partner in Levett-Therivel consultants, who specialise in sustainable development policy, appraisal and management. His previous work includes *What Counts for Quality of Life?* (UK Round Table on Sustainable Development, 2000), *Greening Economic Development* (Local Government Management Board, 1993) and *It's Not Just the Economy, Stupid* (CPRE forthcoming), work on quality of life capital and sustainable settlements, and the sustainability appraisals of numerous plans and strategies.

Ian Christie

Ian Christie is an associate of the New Economics Foundation and of the international online magazine and forum www.openDemocracy.net. His publications include the second Real World Coalition book *From Here to Sustainability* (Earthscan, 2001, with Diane Warburton).

Michael Jacobs

Michael Jacobs is General Secretary of the Fabian Society until October 2003. An environmental economist, his books and pamphlets in this field include *The Green Economy* (Pluto, 1991), *Greening the Millennium: The New Politics of the Environment* (ed; Blackwell 1997) and *Environmental Modernisation: The New Labour Agenda* (Fabian Society 1998).

Riki Therivel

Riki Therivel is a partner of Levett-Therivel and a visiting professor at the School of Planning, Oxford Brookes University. Her specialist expertise is in sustainability appraisal and strategic environmental assessment, on which she has worked with a wide range of public bodies, particularly in the land use planning field.

Acknowledgements

This report is the product of a research project undertaken by the Fabian Society with Levett-Therivel for the UK Sustainable Development Commission. The Commission's own conclusions from the research and its work programme in this field can be seen at www.sd-commission.gov.uk. We are grateful to the Sustainable Development Commission for inviting us to do this work. We would like to thank the Sustainable Development Commissioners, invited external reviewers and the Commission's staff involved in the project for their incisive and challenging engagement. They are not responsible however for the final outcome. We.would also like to acknowledge our debt to other thinkers in this field, particularly Herman Daly, Manfred Max-Neef, Tony Clayton, Paul Ekins, Tim Jackson and Nic Marks, whose ideas we have found immensely illuminating – although this is not to claim that any of them would necessarily endorse all the uses to which we have put their ideas here.

Summary

This report was commissioned by the UK Government's Sustainable Development Commission, which asked the Fabian Society with Levett-Therivel to look at ways of increasing wellbeing while reducing environmental damage.

Sustainable development is a challenge to improve the quality of life while living within environmental limits. Government policy has been mainly aimed at increasing the 'resource productivity' or 'eco-efficiency' of the economy through technological innovation. But improvements in efficiency are partly or completely cancelled out by economic growth – caused in part by those very efficiency gains. The result is that for key environmental impacts we are at best running to stand still.

The big issues are therefore economic growth and consumption. Consumption has been largely taboo because of the importance given to 'consumer choice' and the relative underdevelopment of policy thinking about quality of life and life satisfaction.

The report argues against the standard assumption that economic growth is good in itself because it increases consumption choices and individual utility. Measures of national welfare suggest that rising GDP in developed countries, including the UK, may now be associated with declining wellbeing. Choice and consumption bring both benefits and problems. Understanding them allows us to 'decouple' the idea of enhancing wellbeing from that of boosting consumption.

To understand the relationship between consumption and wellbeing the report suggests a model of the different kinds of benefits – subsistence, experience, belonging and self-actualisation – which goods and services provide. Appetites for subsistence and physical comfort are eventually sated. However consumption also has important social and cultural dimensions. People define themselves and their relationships with others through consumption choices. But here too there are limits to the wellbeing which increased consumption provides.

Life satisfaction research shows that wellbeing depends on an individual's situation relative to his or her own expectations and in comparison with others. More and more consumption is now a search for 'positional' goods – those whose value derives from their scarcity, such as houses in fashionable areas and exotic holidays – which cannot be universally available. Advertising is frequently designed to increase dissatisfaction in order to drive consumption. As collective service provision is reduced, new consumption patterns can deepen the absolute as well as the relative disadvantage of the poor.

The report argues that the capacity and opportunity to make fulfilling use of time should be given more prominence in decisions about consumption. A 'fast-moving' modern lifestyle, rushing between fragmented and commoditised transactions, may be less satisfying than one in which material, social, emotional and creative needs are satisfied simultaneously in apparently slower and duller – but actually richer and more multi-layered – ways.

At the heart of the report lies an interrogation of the concept of 'choice'. The concept of consumer choice has become a key principle for economic policy and, increasingly, for policy towards public services. It is assumed that greater choice automatically increases wellbeing. But the report rejects this view. It argues that the consumer economy's dazzling success at expanding one kind of choice – the variety of consumer goods on offer to those with the money to buy them – comes at the expense of restricting other kinds of choice, notably about public and social goods. It can also increase the deprivation of the poor.

There are no 'free choices'. Every choice is constrained by the context in which it takes place. Making some choices possible precludes others. The report introduces the concept of choice sets – the 'package deals' of interconnected acts of consumption which are available given particular infrastructures and market conditions.

Current choice sets in many fields are environmentally unsustainable and socially undesirable, providing individual consumer choice while excluding different kinds of social and individual benefits. Increasing choice within existing choice sets does not necessarily therefore increase wellbeing. The report gives examples from transport, food/agriculture, parental choice in schools, pensions and other areas.

Claiming that a policy or decision 'increases choice' should therefore be the beginning, not the end, of debate. The report argues that what is needed is not more of the same kind of choice, but instead a conscious decision about which kinds of choices really matter. Society needs a better choice of choice.

The alternatives are not just the current model of consumer choice versus a 'hair-shirt' notion of green living. Through policy design we could achieve a richer future with higher quality of life and lower environmental impact. But this will require a more sophisticated treatment of the objectives and direction of economic policy and therefore of the long-term benefits of alternative policies. The report recommends that:

- Policy should be based on explicit quality of life and environmental objectives, not economic proxies for them. In particular, GDP growth should not be treated as an objective or indicator of sustainable development

- Consumer choice should be treated as a means to an end, not as an end in itself. The kinds of choices that policy should aim to increase – including collective choices exercised though political processes, as well as individual choices in markets – should be a matter of explicit debate and decision

- Government intervention should be used to affect the infrastructures and market conditions which constrain and determine alternative options

- In some public services, standards should be recognised as more important than choice and the state a more effective provider than the private sector

The report suggests that possibilities for obviation – making consumption unnecessary – should always be considered first, even before improving efficiency. Efficiency should itself be measured in terms of genuine quality of life and environmental outcomes in the long term. New or expanded provision should be the last not first policy resort.

All this, the report suggests, calls for a rediscovery of some old truths. It is the job of the political process to articulate and negotiate the kind of society we want. It is the job of government to intervene actively in the economy and other realms of policy, to try to achieve it. These tasks cannot be delegated to 'market forces'. The kind of economy we have is itself an important subject for political decision. Its future course is not fixed or inevitable, but depends on the decisions taken now. Government's challenge is to rise to the more ambitious and proactive role which this analysis calls for. Putting sustainable development principles genuinely at the heart of government could join up policy and bring within our grasp the apparently utopian goal of giving everyone a good quality of life while living within environmental limits.

1| The race between eco-efficiency and growth

Introduction

Sustainable development is a challenge to reconcile or integrate human aspirations – 'meeting needs' or 'improving the quality of life' – with the constraints of living within environmental limits and not foreclosing options for future generations. [1]

The British Government's main tactic for achieving this is to encourage competitive markets to bring forward technical innovation to reduce the amount of environmental resources and damage needed to support our comfortable material lifestyles. The two key ideas are 'resource productivity' or 'eco-efficiency' to encapsulate the idea of 'doing more with less', and 'environmental modernisation', to establish a link with the Government's almost totemic broader commitment to 'modernisation'.

But how far can this really take us? This chapter starts by noting evidence that over recent decades there have been great strides in eco-efficiency, but they have at best just kept pace with increases in consumption. Of course the future will not necessarily be like the past, but expecting eco-efficiency to do much better in the future would seem to call for some explanation as to why the future should be markedly different from the past: why should there suddenly now be a 'step change' in the rate that technological innovation leads to environmental savings.

One fashionable answer is that the 'new' or 'digital' economy is indeed causing a step change in the rate of technical innovation for which history provides no precedent. However after the dotcom hype there seems to be no hard evidence either that the 'digital economy' is qualitatively different from previous waves of technological innovation or that the innovations it brings are automatically or necessarily good for the environment. Nor is there any reason to suppose that the 'new economy' is immune to any of the reasons that eco-efficiency improvements have been wiped out by increases in consumption up to now, notably the 'rebound effect', where reducing the resource costs of producing a good tends to reduce its price, encouraging people to buy more of it. The chapter concludes that eco-efficiency is not enough: that serious policy for sustainable development must also tackle consumption.

The race

Human impacts on the environment are determined by a race between economic (and population) growth and efficiency improvements. Growth means increasing consumption of traded goods and services. All things being equal, this adds to environmental loads and demands.[2] In competitive markets we can expect the economy to get progressively more production per unit of environmental impact because, all things being equal (again!) a company that can produce the same amount of output with less inputs and waste will reduce its costs and therefore be more profitable.[3]

Which trend is winning in the UK?[4] Some dramatic step change improvements have been achieved. Since 1970 many polluting emissions have been dramatically cut (though some are now creeping up again, albeit from a much lower base level, because of growth).

For the most important impact, greenhouse gas emissions, the race so far is a dead heat: efficiency improvements are just about keeping pace with increases in consumption. In road and air transport, efficiency is not achieving even this: increases in consumption are outrunning efficiency improvements. Even with predicted increases in the fuel efficiency of passenger planes, predicted increases in the UK's air traffic would offset between 30 per cent and 50 per cent of the UK's committed emissions reductions under the Kyoto protocol; a fact which gets less attention than it deserves owing to the continued success of the air lobby in keeping air travel out of the Kyoto process.

The response

The most politically popular and acceptable response to this stalemate has been to urge efficiency improvements to run faster, to outstrip growth. This is the basis of the 'environmental modernisation' and 'factor ten' movements, DTI's sustainable development strategy, the Performance and Innovation Unit report on resource productivity and Tony Blair's 'green speeches' in 2000 and 2001. The political attraction of this approach to the pursuit of sustainable development is obvious. One of the hardest tasks any democratically elected politician can be asked to perform is to call for curbs on forms of consumption – as witnessed by the extreme difficulty for politicians of all parties in facing up to the problems of road congestion and in accepting arguments from advisors for the introduction of road pricing schemes. It is far more attractive to concentrate efforts to achieve more sustainable development on the supply side, seeking technological changes that improve efficiency of resource use, than it is to confront problems of demand management.

There is only one major problem with this. There is no hard, evidence-based reason for expecting – or even hoping – that the relationship between efficiency improvement and growth, which over the last 30 years has been very close to 1:1, should over the next 30 or even 50 years become 10:1 or even 4:1 instead - the kind of factor improvements which sustainability requires. The following sections outline some reasons why it would be mistaken to rely too much on resource productivity.

Where has resource productivity succeeded?

The environmental impacts where efficiency improvements have 'won' are all incidental by-products of economic activity. Nobody wanted sulphur emissions as a result of coal burning, ozone depletion as a result of foam expansion or refrigeration, NOx and CO as a result of driving. Technical fixes for these did not alter the 'core' economic activity.

But space heat and motive power intrinsically involve energy conversion; high speed passenger transport inescapably involves vehicles moving at speed on either ground or air; buildings and infrastructure intrinsically occupy land. Apart from renewable energy sources (which raise local environmental problems) there are few purely technical ways to deliver these economic activities with step change reductions in environmental impacts, because the environmental impact is intimately bound up in the activity itself. This is part of the reason why growth does not automatically become greener.[5]

The new economy

It has been claimed[6] that the 'new' economy[7] can bring a 'step change' in eco-efficiency. This is a field in which hype outstrips evidence. However such evidence as we do have[8] suggests that 'weightless' activity generally occurs as well as 'old' or 'heavy' activity rather than instead of it; that the behavioural changes it makes possible often increase other areas of consumption; and that rebound and behavioural effects can add to environmental loadings as readily as reduce them. The technologies which were supposed to achieve the 'paperless office' actually increase paper use by reducing the cost and time disincentives to endless redrafting and indiscriminate copying. The small body of real evidence yet available suggests that, likewise, better information technologies are increasing the appetite for face-to-face business meetings rather than replacing them. This is in line with historical evidence – the growth in physical transport over the last 150 years has taken place in tandem with the growth of telecommunications technologies, and one has fed off the other.

As dotcom hysteria subsides, observers with a sense of historical perspective may conclude that the spread of digital technologies is evolutionary rather than revolutionary, and arguably less transformative or epoch-making than (for example) antisepsis, fossil fuel engines, printing or broadcasting. There is no evidence that digital technologies will of themselves significantly change the environmental intensity of the economy. They could enable social and/or behavioural changes to reduce environmental intensity – but for this to happen they will need to be applied in a policy context that supports this overall goal. There is no intrinsic drive in the digital economy in the direction of sustainable development.

What kind of productivity does the market encourage?

In a competitive market any producer who can find a way to get more production for the same costs will do better and so, over time, production tends to get more efficient. But the measure of productivity that matters to companies is total factor productivity - that is, the ratio of money costs of production to money value of sales. This is not the same as environmental resource productivity. Indeed, the two can pull in opposite directions.

For example, it is commercially advantageous for a company to use a cheap factor of production less efficiently if doing so enables it to use an expensive factor of production more efficiently. High labour costs and low motoring costs, for instance, make it sensible for companies to encourage employees to drive around much more than is socially or environmentally desirable. Over the last century, British agriculture became more cost-efficient by substituting increasingly expensive labour with relatively cheap petroleum fuels and artificial fertilisers. Farms which lagged in following this trend tended to go out of business. Moreover, if market demand is shifting to intrinsically less resource efficient products, companies must respond. When electric typewriters replaced manual ones, and then word processing computers replaced electric typewriters, companies that concentrated on perfecting the outgoing (more resource efficient) technologies went bust.

There is no guarantee that the market's reward to commercial productivity will improve resource productivity. For as long as environmental resources and impacts are cheap compared to other factors of production such as labour and capital, companies will concentrate on getting more production out of these other factors even if the methods they adopt to do so add to environmental impacts, as often happens with (for example) mechanisation of manual processes, 'just in time' delivery of components and concentration of distribution in a few centres. And they are commercially right to do so. Celebrating the handful of counter-examples is a case of the 'Mississippi fallacy': concentrating on a few little boats struggling upstream while ignoring the vast volume of water pouring downstream.

Does productivity reduce factor use?

The mistaken assumption that 'productivity' will be good for the environment almost by definition is supported by an intriguing inconsistency in the claims made for the effects of different kinds of productivity improvement on the amounts of the factors of production used. Increased capital productivity is argued to be good because it allows more growth, not less capital. Nobody argues that getting more production out of capital should enable us to make do with less capital. On the contrary, it is promoted partly to accelerate wealth creation so we can invest in more capital.

Likewise, supporters of increased labour productivity vehemently deny that it will reduce employment, arguing that by improving competitiveness it will lead to growth which will create new jobs faster than the productivity improvements abolish old ones. This defence of raising labour productivity - that ultimately it will not reduce the amount of labour used in the economy because the efficiency savings will be neutralised by growth – is the exact opposite of the justification claimed made for increasing environmental resource productivity, which is that it will achieve absolute reductions in resource use despite helping economic growth. The 'rebound' effects relied on to justify increasing capital and labour productivity are assumed not to happen with resource productivity. The only point of consistency between these apparently contradictory arguments is that they all show productivity improvement to be a good thing: in two cases because it increases use of the factor being used more productively, but in one case because it does the opposite.

Consumption must be reduced

If resource productivity is only running to keep still, that is at least better than being carried backwards, which would happen if consumption growth were not offset by any efficiency improvements. It at least buys time. Clutching at straws is prudent behaviour if it allows a drowning person to keep their head above water for a bit longer. It is only foolish if it distracts the drowning person from reaching for a more substantial support. We should pursue all genuine opportunities to improve resource productivity. But we must recognise that this will only prevent further worsening of grossly unsustainable rates of resource consumption.

To achieve sustainability, and in particular to achieve the deep cuts necessary in emissions of carbon dioxide and other greenhouse gas emissions, the wealthiest third of the world, including the UK, needs to consume less. But we are in deep denial. Challenging consumption is taboo, as noted earlier. The relief and enthusiasm with which politicians and opinion-formers greet every shred of 'eco-sceptic' contrarian science or polemic, every anecdote of resource productivity, every bit of superficial journalistic speculation about the 'weightless economy', shows how desperate we all are to avoid what the evidence is glaringly saying. The next chapter reviews reasons for this.

2| Why reducing consumption is taboo

The previous chapter concluded that resource productivity cannot be expected to deliver sustainable development alone. It will not be enough just to produce and consume more cleverly: we must also consume less. At present, this idea is almost unmentionable in mainstream political discussion. This chapter explores four reasons: difficulties in distinguishing 'needs' from demands, the unchallenged assumption that choice is good, the failure of policy alternatives, and the uneven development of environmental and quality of life thinking.

Difficulty in defining needs

Green thinking has revolved around the idea that consumption should first and foremost be about meeting basic needs. This brings together distributional fairness in the present (meeting basic needs should take priority over catering to unnecessary demands and preferences), responsibility toward the future (safeguarding future people's needs), and sparing use of environmental resources (taking no more than we need). But it suffers from two basic flaws.

Can we really distinguish needs from demands?

First, despite many determined attempts, nobody has yet come up with a generally accepted and persuasive analysis of what 'needs' are. It is obvious that hundreds of millions of people do not have their most basic needs for food, shelter, security and health met, while hundreds of millions of others enjoy material superabundance, and this contrast makes the concept of needs central to campaigns against poverty and for economic and environmental justice.

But between these extremes there is no clear cut-off point where we can say: need is satisfied, from here on we are only dealing with demand. Many studies[9] have shown that 'needs' vary according to the individual and context: that, for instance, some people may be willing to forego food in favour of books, or that one group's 'needs' are another's luxury. And without this, the concept of 'needs' provides little help in guiding policy choices that affect demands and preferences where most people are already well above bare subsistence level.

Is consumption beyond basic needs frivolous?

Second, putting 'needs' on a pedestal implies that consumption beyond the satisfaction of basic 'needs' is unimportant, optional and unnecessary – if not frivolous or downright bad. In saying that the world can provide for 'everyone's need, but not everyone's greed' Gandhi may not have meant that any consumption that does not qualify for the first category must belong to the second. But his aphorism can easily be read this way, and often is.

The great world religions' exhortations to simplicity and poverty have never been taken up by many. Today more than ever, the idea that consumption beyond bare subsistence is meaningless or sterile just doesn't resonate with most people's experience of consumption as important for self-image, positioning in society, and great fun.[10] A big colour digital TV is nicer to watch than a small black and white one plagued by interference. A 2003 BMW is more fun to drive than a 1973 Cortina was. And if it is also more reliable, durable and safe, and less polluting, surely it is progress if BMWs are as affordable now as Cortinas were in 1973. To argue otherwise is to seem a killjoy.

Sovereignty of choice

A second reason why reducing consumption is taboo is the relationship between growth and choice. A great claim of growth is that it gives people more freedom of choice. Giving any individual more money expands the range of choice available to them. They can still do everything they could do previously, but they can also do some new or better things: buying more goods or higher quality ones; getting experiences they could not have before. If by some chance an individual does not want any of these extras, he or she can always put the money by for a rainy day, or even give it away. On this argument, growth is a foolproof one-way bet – if you don't want the benefits it brings, you just refrain from taking advantage of them, it can't bring you any disbenefits either. It's like being given an extra pack to add to your Lego collection. It will probably make you better off because you can make some extra models. It can't make you worse off, because even if you leave all the new pieces in the pile and never use them, you can still make every model you could before.

Linked to this idea of freedom of choice is liberal democracy's clear separation of the 'public' realm where the state has a right and duty to regulate behaviour for the benefit of society from the 'private' realm in which citizens should be free to pursue their own values, preferences and tastes free of interference from the state. Liberal democracies have fundamental principles concerning processes – the marketplace, rule of law and democratic process – but few concerning the judgements to be made about character and lifestyle. Politicians are accused of paternalism or worse when seen to make judgements about (for example) the morality of different religions, or about how people should choose to live (for example family sizes.)

The anxiety to avoid criticism for trespassing on the private realm gives most Government statements and exhortations on (for example) energy, waste or transport a weird one-sidedness, like magnets with north poles but no corresponding south ones: extolling the virtues of energy efficiency, recycling, composting, cycling or public transport, but avoiding any hint of the corresponding criticism of waste of energy, unnecessary rubbish or driving.

The effect is not limited to rhetoric. 'Carrots' for good sustainability behaviour are usually politically acceptable while the corresponding 'sticks' to discourage bad behaviour are always controversial. There is only faint grumbling over huge subsidies for nearly-empty rural bus services. They are 'increasing transport choice' or 'providing a sustainable alternative' which is politically acceptable even if hardly anyone actually avails themselves of the choice, and as a result the buses actually use more fuel per passenger mile than the cars. In contrast, any propose to reduce or restrict parking or charge for road use raises a storm of protest because it 'restricts choice'; or 'interferes with how people want to live their lives': the possibility that such measures might be far more effective in improving the eco-efficiency of transport, cheaper, and more 'economically efficient' as conventionally measured, counts for little in comparison.

Failure of alternatives

A third reason why reducing consumption is taboo is that the last century is very widely seen as a gigantic experiment in which states and political movements based on collectivism and planning for the public good failed, often very nastily, whereas those based on 'freedom' (understood in the sense of maximising the opportunities for individuals to negotiate their own life choices through market mechanisms) 'won'. Democracy, political and social liberty, individual choice and market mechanisms are perceived as going hand in hand.

Uneven development of the debate

A fourth reason that reducing consumption is unknown territory for modern politics is that the 'quality of life' and 'consumption' side of sustainable development has received far less research attention and rigorous investigation than the 'environmental limits' and 'production' side. A great deal of the sustainability policy debate has revolved around questions of the scientific evidence for the effects that human activities have on the environment currently and in the future, and ways of changing production processes in order to make those impacts benign or less damaging. However challenging and contentious the content of this debate is, its form fits into familiar and comforting discourses of science, evidence, technology and managerial responses.

The other side of the challenge – what people's needs are and what could improve their quality of life – is different. There is no piece of measuring equipment that can tell us whether someone's needs are met, or how good their quality of life is. Needs, quality of life and wellbeing are intrinsically normative concepts, of a kind with which our supposedly post-ideological political discourse is not comfortable. Arguing for the primacy of a spiritual or moral dimension can sound like an arrogant or unworldly refusal to engage in normal policy debate – or a tacit admission that sustainable development is not coherent or convincing enough to compete with other political visions.

The result has been an unbalanced development of the debate. There is a huge wealth of data, indicators and indices about environmental impacts, their causes and ways to reduce them. But for quality of life we have little more than an unconvincing scrapbook of slogans, platitudes, vague general exhortations and methodologically inconsistent, partial and anecdotal clues and pointers. When we try to measure the key relationship implied by the two classic definitions, the ratio or conversion factor between quality of life and environmental impacts, we have many different environmental indicators and indices to choose from, but have to resort to crude and simple economic 'place holders' or proxies for quality of life.

In much of the recent debate about resource productivity, there is a vivid contrast between subtle detail about environmental impacts, technologies and the economics of their dissemination and uptake on the one hand, and the simple blanket assumption that contribution to GDP can be assumed to stand for all quality of life on the other. The debate is like a building half completed and coming to an abrupt end with a temporary hoarding on which a crude sketch tries to give some impression of what is still to be built on the muddy and chaotic building site beyond. The task of this report is, as it were, to speed up the building work behind the hoarding: to help our understanding of what makes for quality of life catch up with what has already been done on resource productivity, to allow a more balanced debate about both sides of the challenge.

Conclusion

These points about needs and choice make the critique of prevailing ideas about consumption (and therefore the critique of growth too) look pretty unattractive. It hinges on a firm distinction between essential 'needs' and mere optional, inessential preferences, but we cannot satisfactorily define the former or demarcate the difference. It implies a critical and dismissive attitude to consumption beyond needs which ignores the social role of consumption, denies most people's pleasure in it, and flies in the face of some of our most basic evolutionary programming. It seems to call for restriction of choice and freedom and for a return to economic collectivism whose best-known practical implementations were abject failures in environmental as well as human terms. And we lack a convincing non-consumption-based positive model of wellbeing to set against the ubiquitous consumption-based one.

In contrast, the 'normal' approach sees choice, growth, freedom, consumption and quality of life as all going together. The way leading politicians use them all almost interchangeably only reflects prevailing assumptions. No wonder consumerism wins by default, and many sincere greens think it is more constructive and responsible to try to housetrain its welfare shortcomings through redistribution, and its environmental ones through resource productivity, than to challenge it head-on.

But the relationships between macro- and micro-wellbeing, between consumption and satisfaction, and the idea of choice itself, are actually more complex. The next chapter starts with the relationship between growth and wellbeing.

3| Limits to beneficial consumption

hapter 1 argued that environmental sustainability requires people in the 'developed' world to consume less, because there is no rational basis for expecting technical eco-efficiency to outstrip growth in consumption in future when it has failed to do so in the past. Chapter 2 examined some reasons why the idea of reducing consumption is politically taboo, and suggested that they spring from political and social history rather than rational argument. But this is far from making a case for the social or economic acceptability - let alone desirability - of reducing consumption. The present chapter turns to this. It aims to show why limiting consumption need not be a bad thing by investigating the relationship between consumption and wellbeing in more detail.

Diminishing returns and satiation

Are we programmed to (over)consume?

Our ancestors got evolutionary advantage from eating as much as possible and lazing around when they had the chance - to build fat reserves, rest and recharge to improve their chances of surviving the hard times that were often ahead. In many subsistence societies fat is admired as a sign of distance from starvation. Likewise, throughout history people have taken whatever opportunities they have had to ease off physical labour. The life of idleness and luxury may have been denounced by prophets and sages, but most people envied the lucky few who could have it, and aspired to join them.

This might suggest that greed, gluttony, indolence and love of luxury are programmed into us, and that abstemiousness is unnatural. But even if this is the case, it is not necessarily an argument for letting our appetites rip. Many atavistic human traits which had survival value for our ancestors have become problematic in modern societies and now need to be channelled and managed to enable us to live securely together. There is no reason why this should not also apply to our consumption urges now that, for the first time in human history, a life of physical inactivity, indolence and overeating is within the reach of most people in affluent countries, and is indeed virtually forced on many of their poorer citizens.

Satiation at the individual level: a food metaphor

Consider what happens to individual wellbeing as ability to consume food, one of the most basic prerequisite of life, increases. If you are literally physically starving, any food with any nutritional content is unconditionally good for you - no matter how revolting. (In 1871 the Paris Communards made banquets of roast rat.) If you are a little better off - malnourished but not actually starving - then any food that supplies the nutrients you are short of is good. (The tartness of the lemons Captain Cook made his sailors eat was a very minor consideration compared to their effectiveness in preventing scurvy.) Once you are adequately nourished, then an increase in the freshness, diversity, tastiness and so on of your diet is welcome and pleasant – but nothing like as urgent or important as basic nutrition when you lack it. And if you are already overfed, more food is bad for you: it overloads your digestive system and undermines your comfort, fitness and health.

This example shows first diminishing utility of increments of consumption - the better fed you are, the less benefit further consumption brings, and the more picky you are about the kinds of further consumption that will bring benefits. This is a well-established concept in economics. However one of the basic tenets of 'standard' economics is that demands are limitless: that returns on more consumption will diminish but never actually stop or reverse. The last step in the food sequence contradicts this. This implies that beyond a certain point more consumption not only stops providing benefit but may cause disbenefit; and therefore (whether or not there are limits to growth) there are limits to the desirability of growth.

But does this intuitively plausible idea apply to consumption in general, and in aggregate? Conventional economics would not deny that there are limits to the amount of many individual goods that people can usefully consume. But it would argue that once they have plenty of one good, people will move on to another. Sensible demand for each individual good may be finite, but the range of potential goods people might consume, and of satisfactions from doing so, is limitless. However Wolfgang Sachs et al. suggest that there are limits to the pleasure people can get from things in aggregate, as well as from particular kinds of thing:

'Beyond a certain number, things becomes thieves of time. In a culture where each household - unlike the Navajos with only 236 objects - has an average of 10,000 things at its

disposal, shortage of time must predominate. Goods both large and small have to be chosen, bought, set up, used, experienced, maintained, tidied away, dusted, repaired, stored, and disposed of... The number of possibilities – good, services, events – has exploded in the affluent societies, but the day in its conservative way continues to be limited to 24 hours... An excess of things obstructs everyday existence, distracts attention, dissipates energies, and weakens capacity to find a clear-cut direction'.[11]

Satiation at the social level

Does satiation happen at the level of a whole society, not just for (some) individuals within it? One attempt to construct an index of wellbeing suggests so. The Index of Sustainable Economic Welfare (ISEW) is an attempt to create a better measure of welfare than per capita GDP by adding to it some measure of benefits omitted from it because they are not traded, such as unpaid domestic work, subtracting the value of activities which are traded but do not contribute to human welfare, such as accident repairs and insurances; and corrects for income inequality. The UK's ISEW rose until the mid 1970s, then stayed level and began to decline again, while per capita GDP continued to rise. ISEWs calculated for several other developed countries all show the same overall pattern of levelling off and then decline.

ISEW has rightly been criticised as a methodological mongrel, made by arbitrarily aggregating incommensurable (and often individually questionable) indicators of very different kinds of things. It is only valid to the extent that it encapsulates and reflects peoples' actual perceptions of wellbeing.[12] Between 1996 and 2002 one of the present authors (Roger Levett) carried out 'straw polls' at over 100 conferences and training events involving over 3000 people throughout the UK. When asked to choose which of two lines – GDP rising more or less continuously since 1950, and ISEW, rising until the mid 1970s then stagnating – was closer to reflecting their own perception of how welfare had changed in the UK, on every occasion a majority, and usually a large one, favoured the ISEW. This does not prove anything. But it suggests we should be very cautious about assuming, claiming or implying that rising per capita GDP tells us anything about welfare.

It is hard to validate the ISEW curve against comprehensive studies of perceptions of quality of life more rigorously, since few surveys have been done that measure changes in people's views of their well-being. However, the accumulated data from many theoretical, quantitative and qualitative studies that have examined aspects of quality of life do suggest that the ISEW's picture of a sizeable gap between GDP per capita measures of welfare and 'real life' welfare is on the right lines. Theoretical work has long suggested that beyond an (uncertain) level of affluence there are diminishing returns to personal wealth and to social well-being.[13] The growth in congestion and the demand for more space for housing and traffic, both side-effects of traditional growth and expansion of particular kinds of choice, are experienced by many as a severe harm to their quality of life.[14] Survey data regularly show that there is no straightforward connection between levels of affluence and personal happiness.[15] More financial security does deliver more well-being for the less affluent, and unemployment is a chief cause of unhappiness. But the rich are not reliably made happier by having much more wealth than the rest of us: being healthy and married, in particularly, have been shown to be better paths to happiness.[16]

There is plentiful quantitative and qualitative evidence of a broader issue – that rising average affluence in the West has not been associated with the elimination of many psychic ills. Money can buy us goods and services undreamed of in previous centuries, but it can't buy love or meaning, or at least not for long and not reliably. The pursuit of financial security and 'status consumption' is often associated with declining quality of working and family life in much of the West. There is a large and controversial US literature on the strains on the well-being of family life in both middle and working classes as a result of intensified workplace pressures over the last 20 years.[17]

In the UK, the latest ESRC study on modern employment trends indicates a rising dissatisfaction with working life over the past decade.[18] Oliver James summarises a mass of research on the psychology of affluent societies, concluding that rates of depression, suicide and drug dependence are increasing because the competitive pressures of modern life combine to produce unhappy, tense and rancorous personalities, partly by reducing brain serotonin levels.[19] Various studies have shown that it is the distribution of assets and capabilities that counts for well-being, not absolute levels of income, and documenting the health effects on society of relative deprivation and relative income inequalities.[20]

A further dimension is that the process of growth in a market economy – and especially in an economy open to trade in a globalising system – is based on what the economist Schumpeter termed 'creative destruction', precipitated by technical change, market development and competition. At any point certain markets are shrinking and others growing, and the instability can create many zones of low quality of life within a growing overall 'space' of high quality of life. Thus the pressure on farming has greatly reduced the incomes and quality of life among many farmers at the same time as economic growth and increases in average real income have been substantial. The welfare economist Amartya Sen[21] refers to such processes as the erosion of people's 'entitlements' – in his terminology, the bundles of economic resources over which they can claim control and ownership (such as a job, a salary, loans etc.). Entitlements are more than money and are basic to the potential that people have to lead a fulfilling life. On this analysis, the ISEW also reflects the erosion of entitlements in different parts of the economy as it is subjected to greater international competition and technological change.

These studies and many others suggest that conventional growth produces many unwanted side-effects and is associated with diminishing returns in many respects. Together, these add up to a body of evidence that, while not (yet) associating GDP growth with declines in overall quality of life, does associate it with limits to the satisfactions that can be gained from many forms of consumption growth, and with damage to the social and environmental basis of well-being.

Less is more?

The food metaphor above mixes up quality and quantity. Is it not possible to separate the two - to pursue increases in quality without increases in quantity? Nouvelle cuisine and Japanese food exemplify this, aiming for subtlety and refinement with less volume of consumption. Indeed, as Richard Ballantyne remarked in his classic *Richard's Bicycle Book*, an extra way (beyond the obvious ones) that bicycles are 'green' is that the more you pay, the less you get: the better the bike, the less it weighs.

But areas where it is accepted that 'less is more' are rare and embattled. For every person dreaming of replacing a 13kg bike with a 12kg one, there are thousands dreaming of replacing a 1,300kg car with a 2,000kg four-wheel-drive SUV. Nouvelle cuisine only enjoyed a brief vogue, perhaps because too many people getting up still hungry concluded grumpily that it was a pretentious rip-off. Moreover, minimalist gesture is misleading if based on profligate support services the other side of the baize door. The apparent 'de-materialisation' of a nouvelle meal may be spurious if the tiny amount of exquisite food actually served rests on a concealed pyramid of fuel-profligate air-freighting of exotic ingredients and wastage of the less choice parts. Or if the restaurant is air-conditioned and the patrons arrive by limousine. Or if they detour to a drive-thru McDonald's to fill up afterwards. The pared-down economy in materials in some celebrated iconic Modern Movement buildings left them unable to provide a tolerable living or working environment without vast expense on heating and/or cooling plant, or intrusive energy efficiency retrofit.

It is 'whole system' environmental performance that matters. Hearty meals from local low-technology foods, ornate and opulent buildings with high thermal mass and passive ventilation may be more resource efficient than their apparently leaner alternatives. Resource efficiency need not dictate a cramped, joyless or mean aesthetic. Hugh Fearnley-Whittingstall has a huge following not just because he takes such obvious delight in raising (and eating) his animals but also because the locally-based, 'slow' food he writes about tastes so good. 'Less is more' is striking as a slogan precisely because most of the time we assume that 'more is more'. 'Quality instead of quantity' does not refute the idea of satiation, but is a potential way to allow wellbeing to increase independent of resource consumption - and one which needs support.

The satisfactions from consumption

To explain how consumption can reach a limit – how satiation can occur – we need a more sophisticated understanding of the range of benefits consumption can provide. The conventional model of the economy which we have already invoked is that money buys goods; goods give the people who buy them utility; and more utility makes people happier. People buy goods because they think they will be better off . The amount they pay tells us what the goods are worth to them.

These propositions are nearer to axioms that define money, goods, utility and wellbeing, than observations about reality. But they are used to justify sweeping practical conclusions. Growth is good because it gives people more money to buy more goods. Any interference in consumer choice must by definition reduce utility since it is pushing people away from their optimal choice pattern. Therefore any deviation from the unconstrained market requires specific justification but this ignores some important points:

- It assumes that that utility is static and externally defined. This denies any capacity for belief and value systems and social patterns in influencing what people regard as good, and the role of psychology and sociology in defining goods and utility. The existence of a multi-billion-dollar advertising industry can be seen as a refutation of this assumption, since if it were true, any advertising beyond provision of bare facts would be futile

- The assumption that consumers can have perfect information is ludicrous in a complex economy. The psychology of filtering, cognitive consonance/dissonance, judgements about risk and uncertainty is an indispensable component of any realistic model of consumer decision. (Nor can producers achieve perfect information, even about the resources they are using for production. In some cases the relationship between prices, information and behaviour is extremely tenuous, as shown by the case of over-fishing: fishermen cannot determine the sustainable catch, and limits to harvesting do not show up reliably in the prices of fish, thus giving consumers quite misleading information about the resources and market with which they are dealing)

- People increasingly define themselves by their consumption patterns: what they eat, wear, drive and so on expresses allegiance to some groups, and differentiation from others. Consumption is now widely seen as an act of self-expression - 'I shop therefore I am' – and as a way of positioning individuals in society[22]
- The relationship between utility and happiness is complex. People can be happy with very little wealth/income/possessions, or miserable with plenty
- Common human activities such as gambling on the lottery - apparently totally irrational on a simple literal interpretation of utility - can only be shoehorned into the model by saying that the thrill of the chase or the ability to dream of winning have more 'utility' to the mug punter than other things he/she could have bought with the ticket money. In which case, the concept of 'utility' has no meaning independent of 'the things people choose or want', and therefore no independent explanatory or predictive power. If someone does an apparently silly thing, it must be because it had 'utility' to them. This tells us precisely nothing about their behaviour
- 'The best things in life are free'. Everybody accepts that some of the things that matter most for wellbeing – like health – are not tradable. Everybody also accepts that some kinds of economic activity – like too much alcohol or food – can undermine these untraded benefits. Given diminishing marginal utility from traded activity, it follows logically that at some point(s), further undermining of untraded benefits by traded activity causes more loss of wellbeing than gain. The empirical question is, at what point(s)?

To respond better to these arguments it needs to be acknowledged that consumption provides a range of different kinds of benefits to varying degrees. We propose an expanded model:
- Money buys goods
- Goods provide services
- These services provide several kinds of benefits:
  - subsistence – basic life support
  - experience – for example the sensory pleasure of comfort or eating
  - belonging – expression of a group or collective identity or affiliation
  - self-actualisation - expression of individual identity
- These benefits contribute to human wellbeing and (though indirectly) to happiness

Table 1 gives some examples. This taxonomy – especially the four kinds of benefits – is related to both Max Neef's and Maslow's work.[23] However, we have kept the list of benefits broader and simpler than Max-Neef's table of needs because the points we wish to make do not depend on the (contentious) details. Most of our points are independent of the most contentious aspect of Maslow's work, the question of whether different needs form a hierarchy in which people only start to worry about their 'higher' needs such as self-realisation once 'lower' ones such as comfortable subsistence and security are met. We make no claim that it is rigorous or definitive, and use it simply as a tool for bringing out points we think are significant.

One important aspect of this approach to needs and satisfactions is that we can use it to analyse how there are typically multiple ways to achieve the same benefit – some more effective, and more environment-friendly, than others. This provides a way to explore the alternatives to existing forms of consumption, and to specifying ways of meeting the same needs and wants that they satisfy, with fewer or no damaging side-effects.

Table 1: Expanded model of consumption and quality of life

	Physical goods	Services from goods	Quality of life benefits			
			Subsistence	Experience	Belonging	Self-actualisation
	CD Player	Music reproduction	-	Enjoyment of music	Participation in cultural group	Personal experiment/taste in music
	Washing Machine	Clothes cleaning	Hygiene	Comfort	Compliance with social grooming norms	-
	Clothes	Being clad	Protection against weather	Comfort	Expression of group identity	Express individual taste
	Car	Mobility: controlled environment	Access to life support basics	Comfort, power, isolation	Expression of status; membership of 'haves'	Autonomy and choice of access
Spending power	Food	Eating	Nutrition, support to health	Taste, pleasure in eating	Cultural/traditional/religious affiliation	Enjoyment of different tastes
	House	Space for living and storing possessions	Shelter, security	Comfort, convenience, delight	Neighbourhood, way of life	Architectural taste

Happiness

Alternative ways of providing wellbeing

The first significant point the model implies is that consumption of traded goods and services is only one of a number of possible sources of wellbeing. Wellbeing does not come only from traded goods: goods can be given, taken, bartered or made as well as bought and sold. More money does not necessarily mean more benefits. This is one of the main reasons economic growth is a poor measure of welfare. For example GDP goes up if a couple divorce and then have to buy in the open market (and earn enough to pay for) services they used to provide each other for free - childcare, DIY, housework, sex. A tightly knit community where people look out for each other and do each other errands and favours may provide more quality of life benefits than a richer society where people have to spend more on buying such community services because social networks are weak. This is also the reason why cash income is a particularly unreliable measure of the wealth or poverty of people in transition from traditional (largely cashless) subsistence/barter economies to market economies, as discussed later in this chapter.

Over recent years, there has been a trend to replace many services previously provided by people to each other – cooking, washing, cleaning, repairing, story-telling, playing music – by commoditised, mechanised versions - ready-prepared food, mechanical cleaning, recorded speech and music. This may improve the service – Stephen Fry reads Harry Potter books better than most dads; Marks and Spencer food technologists often produce a tastier (and also more authentic) version of many dishes than most people could cook for themselves. This may also improve 'subsistence' and 'experience' benefits. But 'belonging' and 'self-actualisation' bene-fits are different. Your own dad may be a shambling, hesitant and thoroughly infe-rior reader of Harry Potter books, but he's there, sitting on the end of your bed, doing it for you, discovering it with you and noticing when you're drowsy and it's time to stop reading, tuck you up and turn the light off. No tape or video does this. More expenditure on story tapes may signify an impoverishment of family life.

Ken Peattie[24] commented to us that:

'If evidence from psychology suggest that satisfaction comes from forming satisfactory relationships, then increasing consumption may actually erode our satisfaction and well-being if it increasingly isolates us. Henley Centre research has suggested that consumption trends are tending to isolate people. Once families viewed TV programmes together, but now videos and multiple sets encourages individual viewing at different times or in different rooms. Convenience foods and microwaves have reduced the need for families to sit down and eat together. PC games have reduced the need for children to play together. Therefore consumption activities may actually be displacing activities from which important forms of *satisfaction are drawn. This is along the lines of Ivan Illych's "Modernised Poverty" concept.'*

However, there is another side to this. Family members might not regret the isolating tendencies mentioned in the above example, especially if people have grown up with no memory of alternative arrangements, or associate close family bonds with unhappiness, lack of freedom, violence, etc. Many people prefer to live in a looser and more open society in which access to services does not depend on one's social relations with neighbours one may not like. Washing machines, dishwashers and such like may free people (mostly women) from tedious chores (although if there is a rebound towards higher expectations - for example outer clothes freshly washed every day rather than going several days - the net time saving may be reduced.) The point is that relationship between spending, consumption and wellbeing is complex: we cannot assume that more consumption inevitably means more wellbeing. Moreover, there is no avoiding judgements about the desirability of different relationships, and making an ethical statement about what kinds of consumption we think should be encouraged and discouraged.

Eco-efficiency

The second important point that emerges from Table 1 is about eco-efficiency. The variable relationship between money and goods (and *a fortiori* between money and services or benefits) means that measuring resource productivity in terms of environmental inputs per unit of traded economic activity is inadequate, because there are so many conversion factors between the two. As a partial example of this, consider energy efficiency in housing.

The Building Regulations (and the computer model of energy performance they use) set standards in terms of heat loss per area of exterior walls, roof and floors of a house (with some ability to trade off better performance on some elements against worse on others.) This means that a house that throws heat away through having a complicated shape with lots of exposed wall and roof area can score just as well as an efficient plain rectangular one built in the same way. It means that a terraced house – with perhaps less than half the exposed area to lose heat through – scores no better than a detached one. And that a large house with one or two people rattling about in it doesn't score any worse than a house that is efficiently occupied.

Thus the Building Regulations give housebuilders no incentive to choose efficient built forms (for example flats and terraces) or to match built space efficiently to the actual needs of the occupants. It is quite possible for a small household in a brand new Building Regulations-compliant house to be throwing more heat per person away through elaborate bays, dormers, and vast expanses of exposed surface than a larger household in a traditional terraced house whose walls and roof would fall lamentably short – but has much less of them per person.

Different ways of providing benefits can have vastly different levels of environmental consumption if they come from different goods – or not from economic goods at all. For instance, in Table 1, a car provides autonomy. This can also come from buses (provided they are regular, reliable and go where you want), bikes, or having services located close to people. A car also provides an expression of status: arguably this can be provided much more effectively through awards, titles, or other peoples' behaviour. The key case for us to investigate will be ways to get 'belonging' and 'self-actualisation' benefits without consumption, or with significantly different consumption, because there is no logical reason in general why these benefits can't be wholly decoupled from environmental damage.

Satiation revisited

The model of benefits from consumption also allows us to make more explicit the idea of 'having enough' that was implicit in our earlier discussion. Consider the four categories of benefits we have identified:

Our first category of benefit is subsistence – the wherewithal of basic survival. Subsistence needs are determined by human physiology. Humans can only live healthily and comfortably within a narrow range of conditions – ambient temperatures, amounts of different gases present and absent in the air, fresh water, nutrition, protection against the weather, predators, parasites and criminals. Where conditions fall short of these standards, consumption can improve quality of life (for example ability to buy more food, clothing, space heating and to secure one's home and basic possessions.) But once these standards are met, extra consumption provides no extra benefits. There is no subsistence advantage from eating more vitamins than the recommended daily intake, wearing more clothes or heating the house above a healthy comfortable temperature (as shown in the example of food: it can, in fact, reduce wellbeing). From the point of view of subsistence, 'enough is as good as a feast'.

Our second category of benefit is experience. Consumption can keep rising well above subsistence levels and keep providing more comfort and stimulation. Increases in the variety, quality and amounts of food and drink keep increasing pleasure for a long way, and the same goes for many other physical comforts and sensual pleasures. But here again there are ultimately physiological limits. More stimulation encounters diminishing returns. Even the greediest and randiest eventually find their appetites sated. Sensual overindulgence eventually loses its savour and feels like a chore. Orgies and feasts should perhaps be seen not as ways those lucky enough to participate can expand their sensual pleasure without limit, but as desperate attempts to stave off boredom and indifference.

'Moderation in all things' is a precept that not only accepts the inevitability of satiation of material satisfactions, but advocates stopping pursuing them well short of this point. It is the opposite of the glorification of excess that drives consumer capitalism. It sees the popstar's craving to own more expensive cars than he can get round to driving, and buy more clothes than he can wear, as a sad symptom of some lack of fulfilment rather than as a glorious manifestation of success to be celebrated and admired.

It is striking that most British people stayed within a healthy weight range for decades after becoming able to afford vastly more food than nutritionally healthy. This casts doubt on the 'argument from evolution' mentioned earlier, which predicts that people would overeat as soon as they had the chance. It seems that some combination of internal physiological signals, social norms and lifestyle factors such as regular background exercise and cold buildings kept most people's eating roughly in line with their physiological needs. The 'middle way' was the norm. This has only recently been broken down by a malign combination of sedentary and immobile lifestyles, a culture of glorification of excess which has abolished the old social restraints on greed, and a food production and marketing industry able to make the best profits from nutritionally poor and fattening processed foods.

The development of a huge slimming and exercise industry is a further twist to the same problem. Obesity and anorexia are two sides of the same coin: breakdown in normal regulation of food and eating and inability to find a healthy balance, resulting from the denial of moderation and the promotion of unbalanced, obsessive behaviours. The misery of people (especially women) caught in the turbulence between ubiquitous blandishments to eat too much, and oppressive exhortations to diet and exercise, both of them playing on insecurity, pushing people beyond the limits of health and prudence, and demanding that they spend, spend, spend, provides a glaring indictment of the sterility of excess.

So for both our 'lower' two benefits sheer brute physiology imposes 'limits to growth' – points beyond which further increases in consumption produce no further increase in wellbeing. (Most of the world's major belief systems in fact argue that well before this point, increases in consumption coarsen and corrupt human nature.) An 'experience economy' of consumption based on ever more stimulating and exotic holidays, music, reading, virtual reality games, sporting events, multimedia products and so on could be one way of extending the frontiers and producing new gains in well-being. Even here, however, there are some important limits – see Chapter 4 – based on the problems of competition for positional goods such as travel to remote 'unspoilt' places. 'Virtual' experiences might well produce more demand for the real equivalents, and in any case depend on an energy and material base that cannot be indefinitely enlarged.

But what of the two 'higher' benefits from consuming: belonging (group identification) and self actualisation (individual fulfilment)?

Let us start with belonging. Consumption contributes to group identity through having enough, and having the right type, of goods. 'Enough' goes up with wealth. The size and elaboration of car that confers a given social status in a company car park or outside a school has escalated inexorably: people who wish to claim a place in the pecking order by such means have to go upmarket every time they replace their car. Type will vary with fashion, but will also tend to become more expensive as wealth increases. (For example first having a mobile phone, then having one smaller and smaller, then with pictures, now with video etc.) This would appear to be a zero sum game: having the right (expensive) trainers in 2002 probably provides no more sense of group identity than having a pair of (cheaper) Doc Martens in 1980 - and probably less than having a pair of shoes at all in 1900.

'Dress down Fridays', far from freeing staff from group-defining formal dress codes, require them to make an additional set of judgements and decisions about the identity signals they wish to give in a different, parallel framework of conventions. Standard boring 'business dress' and school uniform can be seen as attempts to free people from having to struggle, decide and spend to project identity and affiliation through dress. People may then concentrate exaggerated attention on the tiny degrees of freedom left – buttons of cufflinks, how far down the chest the knot of the school tie dares go. But this shows how far the means of defining identity and affiliation can be decoupled from volume of consumption. Encouraging this decoupling could be a useful measure for sustainability. For example, encouraging much more competition to own distinctive car number plates could provide a means for people still to use cars to express status, but without needing an environmentally profligate car to do it. This may be happening in a very limited way already. Some of the most exclusive plates are on very ordinary cars. This only makes sense if the owners value the (unique, literally exclusive) prestige of the plate higher than the pleasures of having a distinctly better (but not exclusive or conspicuous) car.

To the extent that self-actualisation benefits are dependent on what other people do (ie to the extent that self-actualisation means differentiating oneself from other people), the same applies. The only kinds of benefit which seem potentially unlimited seem to be self actualisation ones that come from challenges one sets oneself: for example to improve one's personal best at some sport, or to play a musical instrument better and better - with the aim not of 'beating' other players but of coming ever closer to one's own potential or to the soul of the music. Consumption obviously plays a role in these - better sporting equipment or musical instruments – but quality takes over from quantity. (All running shoes and cellos are much the same size: better isn't bigger.) And the higher the level of achievement, the more important the performer's ability becomes relative to the equipment. In many sports, the top performers all use near-identical equipment. We compare how Casals, Rostropovich and Tortelier play, not which of them could outbid the other for the 'best' Amati or Stradivari cello. (Casals, widely regarded as the last century's greatest cellist, was pretty relaxed about equipment: he was known calmly to tie a knot in a broken string and carry on playing.)

Multiple benefits from one object

One of the most important points Table 1 brings out is that a single act of consumption may produce a range of different benefits. If we want to change particular consumption patterns, we need to consider all the benefits – and disbenefits – affected. For example, if we want to encourage less driving, transport policy needs to recognise not only the rational or utilitarian benefits from driving but also the irrational ones – in particular, the extraordinary degree to which social status, economic success and personal potency are now symbolised and expressed by possessing and flaunting particular types and brands of car. Gatersleben and Vlek showed that, of five household goods – car, washing machine, heating equipment, cooking equipment and television – the car contributed most to quality of life because of this.[25] This does not mean it is impossible ever to reduce car use, but instead that, to succeed, 'rational' transport policy aimed at reducing the objective incentives to drive needs to be accompanied by quite different kinds of policy intervention designed to alter perceptions of cars and provide alternative sources of the irrational / subjective benefits currently attached to the car.

Status symbols

Humans have always wanted status symbols. They have often not been goods (scalps, slaves, 'arm candy', ability to dominate and exploit other people). It would be futile to try to stop people having status symbols. But we can instead try to shift the aspiration onto less perilous and damaging objects.

For instance, consider the case of the car. For most of human history people got by without having a private, self-powered conveyance waiting outside every home. It would be an extraordinary failure of imagination to conclude that we could not do so again. But it would also be a mistake to assume that it could be done as easily and rationally as persuading people to switch from coal to gas heating or put composters in their gardens. For this is the first period in human history where a large proportion of people all over the world crave one particular status symbol and where on current trends the economy is going to let most of them get it and where the result imperils our future as well as causing huge social and environmental damage in the present. Ancient myths and stories are full of magical conveyances that transport people with uncanny speed and effortlessness. The car is not a new invention at all, but only the long-delayed and long-yearned-for technological realisation of an ancient and atavistic dream.

Moreover, these magical conveyances were the preserve of gods, wizards and heroes who alone possessed the secret of their operation and the skill and daring to pilot them. So today's paunchy middle-aged sports car buyer automatically assumes a heroic mantle with more resonance and prestige than the most brilliant advertising agency could have concocted. (Car selling is even more blatantly parasitic on the more recent mythology of the cowboy.) Add to this the visceral thrill of speed and danger and the opportunity to show off skill and prowess conquering it, and apparently irrational car worship becomes less puzzling.

But paradoxically the success of the car may offer opportunities to escape its lure. The cognitive dissonance between the free, open, rugged remote imagery of car advertisements and the tedious congested stop-start reality of most day to day driving must surely make the idea of the car as an expression of freedom harder to maintain. Crowded roads reduce opportunities for speed. Even ordinary cars have performance far exceeding the ability of most drivers to use it, while the quality of car engineering has de-skilled driving: steering, handling, brakes, gearboxes and engines have all been made so forgiving that people can get away with appallingly inept and clumsy driving technique without visible problems (to the point where disembodied female voices remind drivers to close doors and fasten seatbelts) and therefore skilful driving provides little gratification. All this has made the experience of driving frequently frustrating, time-wasting and banal – perhaps these are the makings of a counter-mythology? Increasingly, as the inevitable 'social limits to growth' in car use begin to bite in the form of congestion and frustration, it could be not so much the pleasures of motoring that keep people wedded to the car but the perceived and actual shortcomings of all the alternatives to car-based travel.

Demeaning signals

Another useful step might be to correct the subliminal, unintentional but none the less potent signals of disrespect and low status that are projected by other transport modes. The squalor, inconvenience and unreliability of much public transport gives not only a rational disincentive to use it, but also a message that users are second class citizens whose time, convenience and comfort do not matter. It is no surprise that this gives many of those forced to use public transport a burning ambition to get a car as soon as they can for the sake of self-respect, even if doing so makes little practical or financial sense.

Likewise, the careless, half-hearted and patronising design, implementation and management of much cycling infrastructure paradoxically projects a more condescending and demeaning attitude than the previous lack of provision. Cycle lanes parked on, driven in, left strewn with broken glass, meandering round long detours, ending abruptly at the dangerous junctions where they are most needed, interrupted by 'cyclists dismount' signs or traffic lights with inordinate delays at road crossings, and closed and dug up for street works without even the warning signs and alternative routes provided for pedestrians, all project an attitude that cyclists are second-class road users, deserving only marginal (in all senses of the word) provision which is withdrawn the instant it might inconvenience more important people, ie car drivers.

No wonder many urban cyclists respond with the defiance and aggression characteristic of an embattled rebel minority. It may be no accident that many urban cyclists behave worse now – jumping traffic lights, cycling on pavements, etc – than they did a decade or two ago when they were not given any special provision, but not treated with any less dignity than car drivers either. It might be revealing to compare cycling attitudes and behaviours in British cities with Dutch, Danish or German equivalents where cycle provision is not only much better in practical terms, but also projects an attitude of respect and (for example in shared cycle/pedestrian paths) an assumption and expectation of responsible and considerate behaviour which cyclists generally appear to live up to.

Conclusion

This chapter has barely scratched the surface of the psychology and sociology of consumption. But it will have served its purpose if it illustrates that the relationship between consumption and wellbeing is complex and only partly rational and practical. To the extent that consumption is concerned with meeting practical needs, it is possible to mount rational arguments that we would be as well off, in many cases better off, with less of it. Eating too much over-processed food and being too dependent on cars are obvious examples. But to the extent that consumption is 'irrationally' bound up with matters of status, image and perception, this does not mean that it is beyond the possibility of policy intervention.

Instead it means that interventions must be at the level of meanings and values. For example, to persuade significant numbers of 'normal' people to shift from their

Table 2: Different viewpoints on consumption

| Viewpoint | Role in this viewpoint | | | Response to environment | Problems |
	Consumers	Producers	Government		
Neoclassical economics	... are king. Express their preferences through market demand	Respond to market demand by producing what consumers want	Polices the legal framework for the market but sees other intervention as 'distorting'	Old: assumed infinite. New: market will correct problems if property rights defined	Private sector and unregulated market do not operate perfectly as theory suggests
Traditional socialism	Everyone has basic needs which government may understand better than public. Demands beyond this are secondary	Private sector creates demand and sells whatever is profitable, irrespective of real need or social value. Public sector, free of profit motive, meets needs	Intervenes to ensure real needs met, often through public services. Regulates private sector to protect consumers and workers	Old: assumed infinite. Some remaining practitioners (eg Cuba) now show that central planning can respond to environmental scarcity	Lack of market feedback or incentives for entrepreneurship lead to inefficiency, low quality and lack of innovation
Green consumer	Consumers drive environmental improvement by demanding greener products	Respond to green consumer demand by producing greener products	Educates consumers, and supports business greening through (eg) R&D; training; innovation support	Consumers (encouraged but not forced by government) ensure that businesses prosper only by behaving sustainably	Consumers face restricted 'choice sets' and prisoner's dilemma problems prevent collective action
Postmodern consumerism	Construct identities and affiliations through non-utilitarian consumption choices	Enrich consumers' lives and help them construct meaning through brands and product identities	No role beyond guardian of minimum standards	Ignored - except as a possible dimension of chic self-image	Trivial and cannot respond to the environment
Sustainable (as proposed in this report)	Construct identities and meet desires within options created by previous choices and interventions. Suppress desires (eg environmental) too hard to implement	Service consumer identities and demand. Can manipulate perceptions and preferences within the choice sets currently practicable; but very little ability to shift the boundaries.	Huge potential and responsibility to influence choice sets available to consumers and producers through market interventions, infrastructure, etc	Can be protected if government creates market conditions, infrastructures, etc, but not otherwise	Requires ambitious, coordinated and sustained interventions by government and more sophisticated awareness of producers and consumers

cars back to public transport, it will not be sufficient merely to make the public transport cheap, frequent, reliable and comfortable (daunting as those requirements are!) and provide some disincentives to travel routinely by car; it will also be necessary to re-establish the idea that travelling by public transport is a dignified and sensible choice, something that 'normal' people will do routinely as part of a successful lifestyle, not merely a last resort.

4| Absolute and relative wealth

Introduction

The previous chapter reviewed a range of reasons why the wellbeing that individuals get from consumption may taper off and even decrease beyond certain levels of consumption. This chapter examines another set of reasons why increased consumption may not produce the expected levels of wellbeing: the ways that the benefits of wealth to any one person depend on what happens to everyone else, and the ways people's perceptions can be manipulated, for example by marketing. (We are grateful to Ken Peattie for pointing several of these out.)

The benefit of wealth to one person depends what happens to others

One of the more consistent conclusions of the literature on life satisfaction and happiness is the 'Easterlin paradox' that at any given moment wealthier people tend to be happier than poorer people, but that the same people do not generally get happier as they become wealthier over time.[26] The paradix is in fact easy enough to explain. The assumption that growth must increase wellbeing is true if and only if increasing everybody's income has the same effect for all of them as increasing one person's income does for that person. But this is a 'fallacy of composition'. In fact the benefit any individual gets from more money depends on what happens to everyone else:

'absolute income... shows no sign of being positively correlated with job satisfaction... satisfaction... is... more strongly correlated with relative income than absolute income (i.e. the person's income compared to the income that a typical person with the same characteristics would receive).... Higher relative income seems to bring well-being'.[27]

Raising one person's income moves them up the income 'pecking order'. It increases their ability to acquire more for 'exclusive' (revealing term!) goods. This is one reason why pay relativities are often fought over more bitterly than absolute levels.

In contrast, raising everybody's income in equal proportion will by definition make no difference either to people's position in the pecking order or to their relative buying power. It will raise their absolute buying power. But if they were already at or near satiation for subsistence and comfort benefits, this may bring them no more of these benefits, and as we have just argued, belonging and self-actualisation benefits depend on relative not absolute buying power. Even the most naked slogan of consumerism –'the guy with the most stuff when he dies wins' – is about relative consumption – it's having more than others that counts, not the actual amount.[28]

Comparisons between countries tend to support this. In almost all countries, satisfaction surveys reveal that the wealthiest third of the population are happier than the middle third, who in turn are typically more satisfied with their lot than the poorest third. However, the richest third of Costa Ricans are happier with their lot than the poorest third of Germans, despite being poorer in terms of average GDP per capita. It seems that where you perceive yourself to be on the ladder is more important than what you consume in an absolute sense. Or that satisfaction depends on factors that tend to go with higher income, such as quality and interest of work, or having the opportunity for fulfilling social relationships, rather than with consumption itself. (Chapter 7 picks up this theme in relation to time.)

The 'Mr Toad' effect

Contentment may also depend on what one thinks is available or possible. In *The Wind in the Willows* Mr Toad is expansively happy with a boat until he sees a horse-drawn caravan, and then blissful about the caravan until he sees a car, whereupon the caravan is scorned and he has to have a car. And this effect is not limited to amphibians. The story goes that Diderot was given a new red dressing gown as a present, but because it made the rest of his study look shabby he gradually replaced desk, curtains and other things so that they might complement his red robe:[29]

'Subjective satisfaction with one's life is strongly related to one's expectations of it. Expectations in turn are related to social position: people compare themselves to others in their self-perceived social position. Low expectations achieved lead to higher subjective reporting of quality of life than high achievement that fails to meet expectations'.[30]

Ken Peattie reports an experiment that illustrates the same point. 'A group of young children were taken to play in a room full of toys. Each of the toys was incomplete - toy ironing boards without irons, toy telephones without handsets, bats without balls etc. The children were observed. They simply made up for the missing components through their imaginations, miming irons, handsets and so on as they played happily. This process was then repeated with a second group of children of a similar age. But for this group a curtain was drawn back to reveal a glass partition, behind which were complete versions of all the toys that surrounded them. The result was that these children squabbled over the toys, mistreated them, and many ended up with their noses pressed to the glass demanding the 'proper' toys.

People may be perfectly content with the home, furniture, car and so on that they have managed to acquire until some turn of events (for example a legacy) unexpectedly brings bigger and better ones within their buying power, whereupon contentment turns to restlessness, fault-finding and discontent. Contentment may be more to do with feeling one has played one's cards well and achieved a good 'deal' in life relative to one's circumstances and opportunities, than with the actual substance of that deal. Discontent, it seems, comes from feeling that you could do better, rather than from anything intrinsically wrong with what you have got.

Marketing: manufacturing dissatisfaction

Much advertising and marketing is expressly designed to make us dissatisfied with what we have. Cellnet's campaign to make teenagers ashamed of their mobile phones (with the strapline, 'Life's got enough embarrassments, don't let your mobile phone be one of them') is an example of trying to make consumers dispose of durable and technically perfectly adequate goods early.

As we have already pointed out, the neoclassical model of the economy treats consumer demand as sovereign. In this model, marketing cannot create demand, but can only service existing demand or bring to the surface latent demand. Tobacco companies invoke this proposition to defend cigarette advertising on the grounds that it does not encourage people to smoke, but only to switch between brands. If this was the case, severe restrictions on advertising would relieve the manufacturers from having to keep up advertising spend just to defend market share with no prospect of growing the market overall, and would allow them to make larger profits. The way the manufacturers vigorously resist advertising restrictions suggests that they don't really believe that advertising does not create demand.

Another revealing example is the extreme sour-fruit bubblegums marketed in America (brands like 'Warhead' and 'Cry Baby'). When being test marketed, these products were so sour that if you put them in a child's mouth they would simply spit them out. However, once children were exposed to advertising along the lines of 'Only tough kids can chew Warhead' demand was stimulated to the point where the products became some of the fastest growing US confectionery products ever seen. It appears that even our basic human needs and tendencies (if it tastes nasty, spit it out) can be subverted if a product is sold persuasively enough.

Cases like these make claims that marketing merely helps producers to communicate what they have to offer, and thus enable sovereign consumer preferences to direct production more efficiently, look at best naïve where not dishonestly self-serving. The problem is made more urgent by the way that advertising which aims to stimulate demand is rarely targeted so that it reaches only those who can afford a product and who can choose whether or not to consume it. For the marketer, this does not pose a problem, since people who cannot afford the product are not part of the available market, and therefore effectively cease to exist. From a social perspective, it can create a great deal of dissatisfaction, particularly given the increasingly widespread availability of the mass media in very poor countries. People have a greater chance of being happy while being relatively poor if the fact that they are relatively poor isn't pointed out to them every fifteen minutes during commercial breaks.

The difficulty of finding any advertising-free environment in the course of everyday life reinforces the mass exposure to marketing messages, whether people like it or not, or can afford the goods on offer or not. Former French Culture Minister Jack Lang famously denounced Disneyland Paris as 'cultural Chernobyl'. The metaphor might apply even more aptly to western consumer advertising. It spreads a cloud of invisible fallout affecting lives far and wide – a metaphor brilliantly explored in Don DeLillo's acclaimed comic novel on American consumer culture, *White Noise* (1984). Arguably the unpriced social and cultural externalities of Western consumer culture deserve the same recognition, containment and regulation which environmental pollution is now given. Should the appropriate legal category under which some advertising should be considered be not freedom of speech, but conspiracy to secure pecuniary advantage by deception?

Another frequently offered defence of advertising is that consumers have now become so media-savvy, and put up such sophisticated filters and barriers that they are effectively immune to unwanted advertising messages. But this seems unlikely to apply to people in poor countries whose only notion of what western consumer society is really like may come from advertisements, along with the almost equally abstracted and mythologised glimpses of American life in the programmes that separate them. A similar argument could be made in relation to children: although it is often claimed that older children and teenagers are by now (in the West at least) 'marketing-literate' and able to be sceptical about advertising messages, the exposure of young children to a regular diet of advertising images on TV is such that there are serious grounds for concern about their capacity to 'filter' messages. There is growing controversy, for example, over the sexualisation of clothes for under-10 girls, and over the relentless commercialisation of children's TV series and film characters – a debate raised to a new level of seriousness by the intervention in 2002 of the new Archbishop of Canterbury, Rowan Williams, which left *Marketing Week* conceding that his case should give the advertising industry pause for thought.

Distribution

The distribution of growth also makes a big difference to wellbeing. The principle of diminishing marginal returns suggests that the less you have, the more difference each marginal unit of income makes. Any increase in the concentration of wealth will tend to provide less extra benefit to the wealthy than the loss to the poor. The more evenly it is distributed, the more wellbeing a given total of wealth or income is likely to provide.[31]

Moreover, increases in spending power among one part of the population are likely over time to lead to a rearrangement of production and services to respond better to those people's preferences. These changes will not necessarily just leave the poor where they were while others race ahead. They may actively reduce the wellbeing of the poor. For example, as more people become able to afford cars and to drive them further, retailers will tend to respond sensibly by moving to locations easily accessible by car. These will generally be less accessible without a car. Those unable to afford a car will not only experience increasing relative disadvantage through being excluded from whatever additional freedoms and choices the 'great car economy' brings those who can afford to take part in it. They will also find their own access to amenities diminishing, and their living standards declining in absolute terms. Likewise, higher ownership of mobile phones is reducing the financial return on public phone boxes, leading to reduced coverage and reliability.

Positional goods

The limits to the benefits of growth are particularly clear with positional goods – ones which are in their nature finite, or whose value depends on their exclusivity. Hirsch (1976) argues that 'as incomes rise, demand for positional goods increases', leading to rationing (for example by price, entrenching the privilege of the wealth) or to degradation through overuse. Two examples illustrate the consequences. These are given in the following boxes.

An example of positional goods: London house prices

Nice houses in London are a positional good – with a vengeance. Many perfectly ordinary people have woken up to find themselves technically millionaires through nothing more meritorious than having happened to buy a house in London more than a few years ago. But this apparent bonanza of fabulous wealth brings most of them little benefit. For as long as they want to live where they are, the notional value of their house is of no practical use. They can borrow against their equity, but have to pay the loans back if they want to maintain their equity to secure their children's place on the housing ladder. A few cash in their semis in Hounslow for castles in the Scottish Borders or mansions in Somerset. But most do not, because job, income, family, roots and/or lifestyle preference keeps them in London, or because they know differential property price rises would lock them out of returning. High prices make moving within London harder, by increasing both price differentials and many of the costs of moving, which are pegged to property prices.

But if the high prices are little benefit even to owners, they are a nightmare for anyone not already on the property ladder. Inability to afford decent accommodation is a huge problem for younger people and public service workers. Problems recruiting and retaining 'key workers' degrade public services for everyone. Current policies respond to the symptoms through 'key worker housing' deals, which in essence encourage people who are good risks to shoulder even bigger and longer term property responsibilities. Developers argue for release of more greenfield land for housing in the South East to take the pressure off, while environmentalists warn that this will damage quality of life by destroying the few remaining tranquil areas, overload the infrastructure and further worsen the imbalance between economic overheating in the south east and stagnation elsewhere. Both are probably right. But this suggests that action on housing supply is incapable of resolving the problem, and that therefore we need to look at the demand side. In all the furious debate about housing, nobody seems willing to acknowledge that one contributor to the problem is the large number of households with incomes much higher than the average, with which they can bid up the price of desirable housing beyond the reach of people on normal incomes. There are some obvious conclusions – that the quality of life of most Londoners, particularly those on middle to low incomes, might be better if the rich were less rich and if economic activity were less concentrated in London; and that tax and economic development policy could improve London's quality of life by reducing incomes at the top – but these, it seems, are utterly taboo.

An example of positional goods: holiday travel

Well-off people discover a new positional good: long-haul holiday travel to exotic destinations. They then consume it (possibly at considerable inconvenience and discomfort) to show off status. Everyone else only dreams about it. But over time the market responds by increasing supply, by solving technical problems (planes with longer range/higher speeds), reducing costs (jumbo jets) and increasing physical capacity (new airports, concrete high-rise hotels on the idyllic beaches.)

The wealthy then go further afield to maintain exclusivity. And the masses follow as soon as they can, continuing the chase. Successive destinations are discovered, developed, overdeveloped, trashed and abandoned. Are the fugitive rich (having to holiday in really inconvenient, uncomfortable, remote or dangerous places to maintain exclusivity) or the pursuing masses (finding the mystique and glamour evaporating the moment they arrive at each successive destination) really any better off for it? Torremolinos in the 1980s beat Skegness in the 1960s for a beach holiday because of reliable good weather. But Pattaya in the 2000s arguably adds only jetlag, thrombosis risks and exotic bugs to what Torremolinos offered.

Symbols of success change. In northern Europe before the 20th century, suntan was a stigma of having to labour outdoors, and paleness signified privilege. Then lower-status work went indoors to factories, offices and skivvying, and a tan became a sign of privileged freedom to lounge about in the sun. The more accessible sunny holidays became, the deeper the tan a white European needed to suggest privilege (and ambitious ones who could not afford a fortnight in the south of France resorted to sunbeds to keep up appearances.) But once even people on low incomes could afford to spend longer out under a hotter sun than was healthy or prudent, the tan lost its cachet and pallor became (at least intermittently) fashionable again.

Consumption, income and wellbeing in different countries

The relation between money and subsistence benefits raises interesting issues about international equity. Measuring absolute poverty in terms of cash incomes can be misleading. If a subsistence economy 'develops', the number of people living below a poverty threshold defined in terms such as $2 a day cash income may fall. But if the development entails subsistence farmers moving into urban slums, they may in fact be less able to satisfy their most basic needs by buying goods and services with cash incomes of more than $2 a day than they were previously through self-sufficiency and mutual collective aid with little or no cash income.

'Purchasing power parity' can only be measured in relation to a given basket of goods or services. Defining the basket is value laden, because people in different places may use different goods to provide the same benefits, and these goods will vary in price in different places. For example, if you want to base your lifestyle around fresh organic fruit and vegetables, fresh air, tranquillity and a vibrant local community, it's possible that you can live better in rural Sri Lanka on $5 a day than in Birmingham on $50 a day. But if you want to base your lifestyle around consumer electronics, Sri Lanka is one of the most expensive places in the world.

If conditions are more hostile, more consumption is needed to achieve comfort levels. People living in Alaska or Siberia need more heat and/or clothing than those living in England. Those living in Qatar need more energy to protect themselves from excessive heat. This raises interesting questions about the meaning of equity, particularly in an environmental context. Should people who live in more hostile environments be morally entitled to more environmental consumption to provide the same level of subsistence benefits? Or do we treat this as a choice they make which the rest of us should not have to environmentally 'cross-subsidise'?

These are unavoidably value-laden questions. Simple economic measures such as cash income cannot give a full picture of differences in quality of life between different places. Even apparently sophisticated ones such as purchasing power parity do not solve the problem.

Conclusion

'Subsistence' and 'experience' benefits eventually hit a satiation point because they ultimately depend on human physiology, and each of us only has so much capacity to eat, drink and feel merry. 'Belonging' benefits from consumption also hit satiation as they become a zero-sum game: growth increases the cost and elaboration of the symbols used for identity, but not what they express. However it is a game that much of the world's population plays, egged on by tradition, competitiveness and advertising. Self-actualisation does not depend on consumption.

More income for all does not increase benefits which depend on people's spending power relative to others' positions. However its consequences can increase the absolute (and not just relative) disadvantage of the least well off, and damage positional goods by increasing pressures on them. Growth now brings continuing positional competition, with diminishing satisfactions in trying to keep up with the Joneses. It leads to a generalised sense of rancour across society among and even against the relative 'losers' – some of whom do their best to keep up in the competition for positional goods through crime. At an individual level, it can even mean doing without items that are not readily observable (like food) so as to be able to pay for visible goods like designer labelled goods or cars, because these in turn determine people's positions in the pecking order.[32] For all the benefits that flow from growth, its domination of the political agenda means that we have a politics that is in large part as Dunn put it 'irritable, reactive and myopic: endlessly saturated with resentment'.[33]

Therefore it cannot be assumed that growth will increase overall welfare. Whether it does so will depend on the starting point, the context, and the kind and distribution of growth. The higher the starting point, and the more unequally distributed the addition, the more likely growth will disadvantage those worst off, ultimately to the extent of reducing overall welfare. The richer and more unequal a society is, the more redistribution and attention to feedback effects is necessary to ensure that growth actually adds to welfare. This seems to imply that – contrary to common assumptions – as an economy grows, more government intervention becomes necessary to ensure that the growth is beneficial, not less. This is discussed more in Chapter 6.

5| Choice sets

Chapter 3 argued that income growth, and extra consumption bought with it, does not necessarily increase wellbeing. This appears to contradict the common sense argument that it must do because otherwise people would not make the choices they do. If we got here through people choosing the consumption they want, surely this must be what they want? This chapter shows why this comforting assumption – which underpins a huge range of current policies - cannot be relied on.

Chapter 4 argued that the benefit extra income brings to any individual depends on what others get. At worst, increased spending power can cause changes in the economy that undercut the benefits people get from it. In the same way, the choices people have already made affect the choices available now. The concept of the individual, sovereign, free choice by a consumer – which lies at the basis of much economic thought – is a fiction. There is no such thing as a perfectly 'free' choice. Every choice is constrained by the context in which it takes place. Making some choices possible precludes others. The choices already made cumulatively alter the availability of choices in the future.

This chapter introduces the idea of the *choice set* – the 'package deal' of choices which are available as a result of a particular set of policies, and which preclude other choices. A choice set is a collection of interconnected acts of consumption, and other behaviours that come with them, and the production and infrastructure that supports them. Each choice set – the choices that are available – comes with a constraint set – the choices and options which it excludes.

Two topical examples are transport and agriculture.

Choice sets: The example of current transport choice set

The current transport 'choice set' maximises:
- Freedom to drive a car wherever and whenever you want. Restrictions, conditions and charges are rare exceptions requiring special justification
- Low (marginal) cost of personal mobility. Once you own a car, you can go a long way in it per pound of expenditure. People with use of a car enjoy extraordinary – historically unprecedented – freedom of mobility
- Ability to get anywhere with a road. The previous two points add up to an enormous freedom to reach locations
- Ability (for those with cars) to choose between competing providers of many services

But these choices preclude others. Very few people can now choose to:
- Live free from traffic noise and pollution and with children able to play safely in front of their homes
- Get access to a satisfactory range of daily amenities on foot without resort to a motorised vehicle
- Walk or cycle to and from their homes with much safety or pleasure
- Make most journeys reliably, without having to make allowance for unpredictable and unavoidable traffic jams and hold-ups

Most households no longer have the option to live a normal full life without owning at least one car. Those who cannot afford a car, or cannot drive because of disability or age, are excluded from areas of normal life, without any choice in the matter. Moreover the patterns of behaviour that result from high car ownership deprive us of other social choices:
- The choice of having vibrant, multifunctional town and city centres. These are threatened both by environmental pollution and congestion in urban areas and by the move to out-of-town centres created by car-based mobility.
- The choice of community vitality. Hypermobility hits poor communities particularly hard, as they often experience the costs – pollution, severance, accidents – of the traffic going through them but not its benefits[34]
- The choice of future climate security. Personal transport accounts for over a quarter of greenhouse emissions and is still rising.

Choice sets: The example of current agriculture

The current food and agriculture choice set exemplified by supermarkets maximises:

- Variety. Supermarket shoppers in developed countries can pick off the shelf every imaginable food from all over the world all year round, and enjoy a range and variety of diet not available even to the very weakest a few decades ago
- Immediacy, flexibility and convenience. All this is available 12, 14 or even 24 hours a day with no forethought or planning
- Cheapness: on many measures, food is more affordable than at any previous time
- Hygiene standards: nearly all food is cleaner and safer than ever before

However this choice set precludes other choices:

- To experience or express any sense of locality, cultural identification or rootedness in place or season though food buying
- To be sure that any food is totally free of genetic or agrochemical contamination, or from unknown new hazards such as BSE, endocrine disrupters and growth hormones. However rare their occurrence eventually turns out to be, these add a whole new type of risk and fear which was not occasioned by the formerly far higher incidence of well known and unchanging risks such as food poisoning
- The ability to support local farmers
- People in developing countries being paid a decent wage and their environment not being damaged by unsustainable (but cheap) agricultural practices
- Security against disruptions to global trade from climate and war

Moreover these choices for the majority with access to a supermarket (which largely means access to a car) deprive the minority without access. Those who cannot drive to a supermarket increasingly experience the opposite to the choices outlined: restricted choice and access, high prices and low food quality.

Choice sets and capabilities

The choice set idea is related to the analysis of well-being, needs and satisfaction offered by the Nobel Prize-winning economist Amartya Sen.[35] Sen argues that commodities need to be distinguished from the characteristics or desirable properties that they supply – in other words, from the benefits and services that they can deliver to consumers. This echoes the analysis given earlier of growth and needs. Sen notes that the access people have to goods and services depends on the 'entitlements' they enjoy – the effective economic resources over which people have control and ownership. But he also shows that the use that people can make of the benefits and services provided by commodities depends, not only on their ability to buy them, but also on the 'capabilities' people have. An individual's capabilities relate to his or her psychological, physical and social characteristics and potential. The greater our set of capabilities, the more freedom we have to derive benefits and services from goods. Both entitlements and capabilities are unevenly distributed in quality and quantity, which places a further major constraint on the consumer's act of choice.

In our terms, capabilities can be related to the idea of 'choice sets'. The goods and services available never come 'neat' - they are bundled up with a whole set of related options and constraints, and are thus intrinsically social. There is no such thing as a purely 'individual' act of choice: we always choose within a choice set.[36] Moreover, in Sen's terms, the extent to which we are in a position to derive happiness or some other fulfilment from a choice set depends on our set of capabilities - characteristics heavily influenced by our wealth, education, literacy, health, location, age etc. Capabilities are of course never purely 'individual' either - they depend on wider social contexts and structures.

Alternative sustainable choice sets

Each of the examples given in the boxes implies an alternative, more sustainable choice set. These have been discussed extensively by the green movement,[37] so this section will give only a brief summary.

The sustainable transport choice set is actually more about spatial planning and service delivery than about transport provision in itself. In it, far more of the amenities and resources people need and want would be available locally or via high quality public transport, so access to amenities is better (and the access penalty of being poor, infirm, old or young much less) even though independent personal mobility is more circumscribed and expensive.

The sustainable food and agriculture choice set would entail more local production and processing; shorter and stronger links between producers and consumers;

better minimum standards of food hygiene, animal welfare and employee treatment (in imports as well as home production); and more options for people to choose higher standards. By involving much tighter restrictions, and possibly complete bans, on 'Pandora's box' technologies – ones which, once released, can never be reversed, notably genetic engineering, it would secure the choice of GM-free and otherwise unadulterated food. It would provide better safety, nutrition and environmental security, at the expense of (perhaps) 30 varieties of sausage in every supermarket, and some ability to tell what season of the year it is from the balance of produce on sale.

Common features

In both of the current choice sets in these examples, individual consumer choice has been made the dominant guide to policy. In terms of overall wellbeing there is no logical reason why the overall benefits of these individually-driven choice sets should outweigh the disbenefits, or the other way round. Indeed this question is probably not capable of 'objective' answer at all. The benefits and disbenefits happen to different people in different ways,[38] so their relative importance is inescapably at least partly a matter of political value.

However there are several reasons to expect that allowing individual consumer preference to dominate policy in areas such as these often produce more disbenefits than benefits:

- The benefits of the current choice set tend to be obvious, conspicuous and immediate. The disbenefits tend to be less obvious, indirect and distant in time and place. So far as decisions are left to individuals, the former are likely to weigh more than the latter
- Both the current choices sets involve high environmental impacts. They increase the 'environment intensity' of access and of nutrition
- Both current choice sets tend to benefit the already well off and disbenefit those already deprived. The exercise of choice by the better off restricts the choices available to the worse off. Both therefore tend to increase inequity and relative deprivation
- Eventually even the wealthiest cannot insulate themselves against the downsides. Nobody – however fabulously rich – can now get from the suburbs to the centre of most British cities as quickly or reliably as most people could in the 1960s. Nobody – however much they are prepared to spend on top quality foods from the most fastidious specialist producers (eg organic, free range, permaculture) – can feel confident they will not fall victim to some new food safety scare that only becomes public when it is too late to take avoiding action, or to genetic,

hormonal or agrochemical pollutants blown in from less scrupulous neighbouring farms

The fact that the policy areas of transport and food/agriculture are currently widely perceived, right across the political spectrum, to be in failure and crisis, is perhaps significant in this respect.

More choice may not leave us better off

In both these cases it looks like we are being given a superabundance of trivial choices while being robbed of far more important ones. Being able to choose from hundreds of different kinds of car, and several brands of coach, train and plane is paltry if as a result it is no longer possible to make straightforward journey by any of these means with confidence of being able to arrive on time and without hassle and effort on the way. This was much more possible 20 or 40 years ago despite (indeed partly because) there was far less choice available: fewer kinds of car, one integrated rail system, one national coach network. It is also partly because far fewer people made such journeys, and this is partly because they cost more in relation to peoples' buying power. There may be a trade-off between two freedoms - ability to afford such journeys, and reliability of arrival. But for the reasons already suggested elsewhere, ability to travel more does itself not necessarily lead to an increase in welfare. Likewise, having 30 different flavours of sausage to choose from in your supermarket does not necessarily make up for not being able to be sure that any of them are totally free of GM ingredients, growth hormones, etc.

Feedback loops

In both cases, apparently innocuous and perfectly rational choices by individuals – to buy and drive cars more as other transport options become less able to provide access to amenities wanted; to go to supermarkets to buy a wider range of more exotic food at lower prices – have led cumulatively to disbenefits which nobody consciously sought. At no stage was an explicit decision taken that the benefits justified the disbenefits. In consciously exercising our individual, incremental choices, we have sleepwalked into some larger choices and foreclosed others without even realising it. The market can be an 'invisible elbow' shoving us into an unwanted corner, rather than Adam Smith's 'invisible hand.'

Individual rational choices do not necessarily add up to the best overall outcome because of the way each choice alters the choices available to others. For example each perfectly sensible choice to make a journey by car instead of bus will slightly:

A Better Choice of Choice

Suboptimal choice: local buses

Local buses show the potential for choice to make us worse off particularly vividly. Deregulation of buses was promised to introduce competition, giving passengers choice, goading complacent former monopoly suppliers to cut costs and become more efficient and responsive to customer preferences and needs to stay in business. Competition did indeed arise, but only on those routes which had high enough passenger flows to offer profits. As elementary microeconomic theory predicted, competing companies added buses to these routes until the ticket income was spread so thinly it only just covered the costs of running the buses, which operators had already cut to the bone, for example by using clapped-out old buses, skimping on maintenance and setting such demanding timetables that drivers had to drive roughly to keep up, and had no slack to accommodate roadworks or other delays.

The result on the popular routes was a proliferation of unwanted choice, a reduction in quality and reliability, and a new traffic problem from a plethora of often dirty and noisy three-quarters-empty buses. And this competition left no profits to cross-subsidise less popular routes, which were therefore cut except where local authorities were able and willing to subsidise them. Loss of these in turn reduced ridership on the popular routes which they fed, often leading to reduced services on them. As a result, bus ridership dropped throughout the UK except in London where services were franchised instead of deregulated and ridership rose. The results of choice and competition were so dire that there has been little protest at a handful of large operators re-establishing near-monopolies in many places, even where the tactics used to drive competitors out have been unfair and unpleasant.

- Reduce the fare income to the buses while increasing the congestion they face, thus making the service a bit less effective
- Reduce the safety and attractiveness of cycling and walking
- Encourage shops and other amenities to move to car-accessible rather than bus-accessible locations
- Encourage better-off people to move out of more heavily trafficked central areas to suburbs with better car access to the new amenities

Each of these changes will encourage more people to switch from bus to car. The cumulative effect of these individually tiny but self-propagating and reinforcing changes is the apparently inexorable trend to urban flight, out-of-town development, increasing car dependency, and (perhaps) overdependent and obese children.

Moreover no exercise of individual choice can reverse this. If a few people become convinced of the error of the current choice set, and switch back from car to bus, they will first have to plan very carefully to work out ways to get access to fragmented locations without a car. Then they will find themselves waiting a long time at the bus stop, breathing in air polluted by all the other people who are (sensibly) still driving their cars, waiting for a bus which has a long service interval (because most people now drive instead) and is often delayed by the cars. The individual choices available within the current choice set cannot solve the problem. This is why 'green consumerism' often makes little difference (and why it is hardly mentioned in this paper). Instead, we need collective action to change the choice set itself.

Choice sets: The example of choice in schools

A further example of several of these points is parental 'choice' in education in the UK. This has been promoted on two grounds: that it fosters diversity; and that the discipline of customers being able to 'exit' will make bad schools improve. But the latter argument is false. Every child is required by law to go to school somewhere, and new schools rarely spring into existence overnight to respond to demand. Therefore 'choice' usually simply reallocates the same children among the same schools. Once a school have become recognised as 'desirable', more families will try to get their children into it. This enables the school to choose which children it wants. (Notice that it is the school, not the families, that actually has the power of choice.) If the school chooses children likely to do well academically, behave well and excel in out-of-school activities, these children are likely to raise the standards still further – motivating more families to try to get in, and giving the school an even better field of applicants from which to choose. An initially small difference can thus easily become magnified into a huge one simply by the rational self interested exercise of individual choice.

Conversely if brighter, better behaved children can desert any school that is seen as undesirable, that school will have to accept more of the children no other schools want. This will make it harder for such a school to improve in either substance or image. A failing pub or chip shop can work hard to improve its 'offer', or it will lose customers and go out of business. A faltering school generally cannot do either – even with an injection of resources from outside. The chil-

---

dren it has had to accept who can't get in to a 'better' school will keep the school unattractive to the 'better' families it would need to enrol to improve, however hard the teachers work. But it will stay open to provide for these children since they have nowhere else to go. Far from making bad schools improve or close, the regime of parental choice tends to make not-particularly-good schools become bad and then stay bad. Only a few schools with extraordinary teaching staff and/or special local circumstances can break out of this feedback stranglehold.

Let us now consider the diversity argument: that choice enables the system to become more diverse and respond to varied needs and demands of different children instead of imposing a grey 'one size fits all' uniformity. How much diversity do people really want, and how much do they get? It is plausible to suggest that 90 per cent of parents want 90 per cent of the same things from a school – a secure and reasonably orderly environment in which every child is able and encouraged to develop their own talents to the full, with staff, resources and equipment adequate to achieve this, and not too far to travel. It is also plausible to suggest that a properly resourced, genuinely comprehensive system with no parental choice at all might come closer to this – giving (say) 80 per cent of the families 80 per cent of what they want – than the current system, which might be characterised as giving 30 per cent of families 80 per cent of what they want (bearing in mind the huge compromises many people currently make over style and ethos of school, travel, even faith, to avoid 'bad' schools) at the expense of giving the other 70 per cent only 30 per cent of what they want.

Human/system interactions

Transport and school choice both illustrate the importance of interactions between people and infrastructure in determining what happens. A metaphor for this is the millennium footbridge in London, the famous 'wobbly bridge' . Engineers had modelled the effect of walkers on the bridge's behaviour, and concluded that with any level of walking traffic the bridge's vibration would stay well within acceptable limits. But they assumed that walkers' behaviour would not be affected by the bridge. They failed to consider whether even a scarcely noticeable oscillation in the bridge might have any effect on the behaviour of people walking on it. What actually happened was that people unconsciously adapted their walking to take account of the oscillation, but in doing so put more energy into the oscillation, making it grow to the alarming levels which forced the bridge's ignominious closure the day after it opened.

Individual versus collective safety

The same problem relates to safety. Safety is widely now construed as a commodity to be purchased individually. Car manufacturers have largely succeeded in framing road safety in terms of buying vehicle technologies. The responsible parent demonstrates love and protectiveness by choosing a massively fortified estate car to take children to school. The wise and mature driver buys a vehicle with defensive cages and crumple zones in all directions, elaborate anti-lock brakes, airbags, wide tyres for more grip, ice warning systems and so on. Even choosing a car capable of double the legal speed limit can be dressed up as a manifestation of masterful preparedness: power in reserve to get out of trouble (implicitly, trouble caused by other drivers), rather than just an outlet for excess testosterone.

The problem with this approach to safety is, again, its effect on others. As research has shown, the safer and more invulnerable drivers feel within their cars, the faster and more dangerously they drive. They therefore take more risks with the lives of people outside. The extra size and weight that makes a car safer for its occupants makes it more dangerous to anyone it hits, since there is more momentum and kinetic energy to dissipate in any collision. Safety by size is another arms race: anyone driving an older, lighter weight car becomes more vulnerable as 'safer' newer cars come onto the roads.

The 'armoured car' approach to road safety also has indirect consequences. Heavier cars use more fuel and thus make more contribution to climate change, which will soon be a life and death issue for millions (albeit remote from the societies where large cars are widely available.) Parents who protect the safety of their children by driving them everywhere store up cardiovascular peril, while parents who make their children get some healthy exercise walking are made to feel dangerous and uncaring.

Local authorities collude, construing road safety as a matter of keeping vulnerable users out of the way behind barriers (adding to both the physical inconvenience and the subliminal disparagement of non-car users). Highways authorities present as a crusade for safety engineering measures to tackle 'accident blackspots' such as straightening out sharp bends and improving driver sightlines – thus enabling drivers to go faster and make more hitherto safe bends and junctions become 'blackspots' in their turn. Road safety driven by 'choice' and 'freedom' is thus a matter of transferring danger and vulnerability from the privileged to the underprivileged, thwarting and demeaning the latter to keep them out of harm's way, and a licence for never-ending investment in trying to keep the high speed safety of roads one jump ahead of the increasing driving speeds which those investments enable.

A Better Choice of Choice

Financial security

Framing financial security as a product to be bought individually leads to equally malign consequences. Fields such as pensions and mortgages are often experienced as 'jungles of confusion' where even diligent research and expensive expert advice can only reduce, not eliminate, the risk of making disastrous mistakes. Even options blessed by the consensus of experts as prudent and low in risk can now go spectacularly wrong, as Equitable Life pension holders have discovered. The choice many people would value above all others - the certainty (not just probability) of financial security in old age - is now only available to a few fortunate minorities who are able to opt out of the vaunted competitive market, such as government employees eligible for the (unfunded) civil service pension scheme.

This further adds to inequality. The well educated, confident and articulate have a better chance of navigating the minefield of choice in (for example) financial services, distinguishing hype from evidence, making valid comparisons between alternatives presented by partisan companies doing their best to prevent objective comparison, knowing when they need expert advice and where to get it, and assessing risks effectively. People who are less well educated, confident and numerically and bureaucratically competent are more likely to be sold a pup by a plausible salesperson – and are the least able to afford mistakes.

Insurance depends on ignorance

Moreover, even if stock markets always rose and financial services were always competently designed, honestly sold and effectively policed, there would remain two fundamental problems with the 'insurance principle' – the idea that people should take responsibility for their own security by making payments to institutions which can cover each subscriber against huge risks and uncertainties by evening them out actuarially over a large customer base. This is a virtually unchallenged axiom of policy: what could be fairer or more reasonable than basing the payout people get in the case of misfortune on the amount they have chosen to pay in premiums?

The first problem is that the public benefit of insurance – of redistributing resources from the people who turn out to be lucky to those who turn out to be unlucky (eg by dying or becoming incapacitated early in the term of a life or sickness policy respectively) – is intrinsically in tension with the commercial interests of insurance companies, which is to predict each customer's risks as precisely as possible in order to reject bad risks (or load their premiums enough to offset the loss) and offer the most competitive premiums possible to good risks while still making a profit.

Until recently, the great majority of life assurance proposals, from people with unexceptional occupations, weights, medical histories and habits, were actuarially indistinguishable and therefore all offered standard rates. People who were already ill or obviously high risk were already excluded: they have always been unable to get life insurance, or only at punitive rates. This mattered less when they could be confident that the welfare state would take care of them (or their dependents).

Two things are now changing. First, the decline in the standard of universal public provision (excused and justified by governments pointing to the availability of private alternatives) has made exclusion from the insurance club calamitous in many cases. Second, technical advances such as genetic mapping and the explosion of lifestyle information available from commercial and public databases and of computing power to collate and analyse it, potentially enables underwriters to appraise every proposer's risk factors far more precisely than would have been imaginable even two decades ago. So far, insurers have generally backed off exploiting these opportunities under civil liberties challenges. But the relative ignorance which enabled insurance to function tolerably well as a public-interest wealth redistribution process administered by private companies is now under threat.

'Can't pay? Can't have!'
Second, a point so obvious that it is easy to forget, is that ability to choose in a commercial market depends on ability to pay. The question of which decisions should be made by individual choice in markets is therefore closely related to the question: which of life's benefits should the rich be able to buy better access to than the poor? In Western consumer societies it is taken for granted that it is right and proper that the rich should be able to buy better housing, smarter clothes, more and newer gadgets and so on. At the other extreme it is generally regarded as unacceptable for wealth to buy political influence (at least at the crude level of 'cash for access' or 'cash for policies'), or exemption from the law. Equal rights of all adults to participate in democratic politics, and equal duties to obey the law, are seen as fundamental to our political system.

Many benefits are somewhere in between – everyone has some minimal entitlement as of right but money buys better. Policy over the last two decades has tended to reduce the minimum standards and make ability to pay more important. Prompt non-emergency health care, education, healthy food and financial security are all increasingly dependent on willingness to pay a significant premium. As Miles put it:

'Consumerism is often more about rhetoric than it is about substance. An increase in the range of choice available to consumers does not always bring with it the resources or the

opportunity to explore such choices at will. The consumer is assumed to be a citizen of a consumer culture, but that citizenship often involves a prohibitive membership fee... Consumerism is not, in effect, an unqualified right. It often has more power to force home to us what we do not have as consumers, than it does to give us what we want.' [39]

Choice isn't always so great anyway

So far this chapter has pointed out several ways that expanding the scope of individual choice can often reduce, rather than always increase, people's ability to get what they want. We should now add that the experience of choice is not the unalloyed pleasure that market theorists assume, but is itself often oppressive, bewildering and a source of unwanted risk and uncertainty. [40]

Having to keep choosing is itself an often unchosen intrusion and demand on time. But anyone who chooses not to spend their time choosing between (for example) energy or telecommunications providers and tariffs or savings accounts, but simply sticks with the one they have already got, is liable to pay well over the odds - particularly as providers of such services now routinely exploit the inertia of existing customers by worsening the terms of old accounts while introducing new ones with better terms to lure new customers [41]. What is presented as lively market competition delivering ever keener deals to consumers actually forces them to spend time continually checking up to avoid being ripped off.

For the same reason, relying on 'green' or 'ethical' consumerism to drive corporate social responsibility or the greening of the economy is:

- Inconsiderate – it requires concerned citizens to spend considerable time on research to put their beliefs into action
- Disempowering and demotivating to the majority who cannot make the time or do not have the research and analytical skills or confidence to do it
- Often more expensive – and thus less attractive – to those individuals who have the good intentions and the energy to identify 'green' choices in the first place
- Ineffective, because only a minority do it

Choice often only offers inadequate compensation in the private realm for loss of benefits of public goods (eg reassuring public spaces). How can an individual 'choose' litter-free streets, good public transport and reassuring routes to school? For many people, the only realm of 'choice' they have is to make private consumption decisions that insulate them from the lack of public goods they experience as a kind of 'fate'.

Choice is also often unsettling. As we have already noted, one source of contentment in life is a feeling that you've played your cards well and got a good 'deal' in life in relation to what you started with. Being given more choices and opportunities may rob your earlier struggles and achievements of meaning. It may make you restless and discontent with your lot in life because of the nagging possibility you could now do better, and make you anxious about making bad choices and possibly doing worse relative to the better opportunities you now have. It would be interesting to investigate whether more recipients of large legacies, lottery wins etc are made less happy for these reasons than are made more happy by their increased wealth.

These examples all underline the relevance of an analysis that treats 'choice' in terms of socially given choice sets and personal 'capabilities'. Expansion of options in given areas of life is only useful if capabilities expand in order to give people the chance to derive benefits from the growth of 'choice'. But there are clear limits to this in terms of people's time, finances, knowledge and ability to influence political and economic decision-making. In some cases personal well-being could even be enhanced by the elimination of the need to choose, and by the security of participating in a choice set of universal one-size-fits-all provision. For example, how many parents would prefer to be able to send their children to the local school, with no choice in the matter, knowing that the education on offer met a national standard of high quality, rather than plunge into the positional competition known as 'parental choice' which so often means 'parental fate' for those unable to move their children in reach of 'good schools'?

6| Time

Time is the ultimate non-renewable resource. Each of us has a finite amount, and what we manage to do with it is arguably the most universal measure of the success of a life. The extent to which our material conditions help and enable us to make what we want of our time is thus a central measure. This chapter offers some tentative thoughts on how this relates to the rest of the argument about consumption and quality of life.

Quality time

Over recent years the idea of 'work-life balance' has entered national debate. This has largely centred on proposals for making working time more flexible to allow parents, particularly mothers, to combine employment and childcare. The underlying acknowledgement is that for many people the different demands on time now run into conflict and have become a source of pressure. But the issue in fact goes well beyond employment practices. Money and time are increasingly out of balance in many aspects of current lifestyles.

There is an apparent paradox which many people have noticed in recent years. We live with ever more 'labour saving', 'time saving' and 'high speed' gadgets. Yet many people nevertheless feel increasingly pressed and rushed; and the newspapers are full of stories reporting increases in exhaustion, stress and nervous ailments from chronic over-commitment and time deprivation. This is happening even as part-time and 'portfolio' lifestyles become fashionable, and more people are earning enough to make less than full time work financially viable. Sachs observes:

'A prime condition for increased social capital is more free time, more sovereignty over time. The less free time someone has, the greater his or her demands of the state and the more

he or she consumes on the market. People can only fulfil services for each other, activate neighbourly relations, and develop forms of immediate solidarity if they have the time.[42]

But there is no simple trade off between time and money. Sheer quantity of time is not an adequate measure of its value. Most unemployed people, and many retired people and others without a clear occupation, find an abundance of uncommitted time depressing and debilitating rather than liberating, even if they are free of the poverty which usually accompanies unemployment. But being obliged to spend time on unwanted and unsatisfying activities is also a privation. Many of the greatest trades union struggles were not about wages in themselves, but about securing limits on the length of the working day to give workers the possibility to do something in their lives more than work, sleep and go to church on Sundays.

On the other hand many people revel in being in demand and under pressure. Stressed and overcommitted people often seem to get more out of their time, and even to have more capacity to take on extra commitments, than under occupied people. ('If you want something done, ask someone busy'). Employment entails obligation to place one's time at an employer's disposal, but is widely felt to be a source of dignity and fulfilment, quite apart from its material rewards.

So we need some notion of 'quality time': time which people are able to use in ways that confer satisfaction and fulfilment. There will be both physical and psychological aspects to this. Hunger, sickness, lack of physical energy will generally reduce people's ability to use time. So will inability to access the places or amenities needed – open spaces for people who get their satisfaction from sport, libraries or concert halls for those with cultural interests and so on. Fear, anxiety, loneliness, anomie and dislocation are also often debilitating although they can also spur some people on. Security, confidence, sense of rootedness in community (whether of interest, faith, ethnicity, or locality) are conducive to ability to enjoy time.

Time and consumption

We could provisionally say 'good consumption' is consumption that removes obstacles to productive use of time. This would include all 'subsistence' consumption and a reasonable (but finite) level of experience consumption. It would also include some 'identification' and 'self realisation' consumption. But beyond a certain point, 'keeping up' with higher levels of these begins to erode time. Choosing, acquiring and servicing possessions takes up time itself; once we are into zero-sum or 'positionality' problems (as described earlier), further increases in consumption crowd out quality time instead of contributing to it. This can be seen as another reflection of the peaking and then decline of the ISEW curve.

An illustration of this is Ivan Illych's famous calculation dividing the number of miles the average American man drove his car each year by the total amount of time he spent earning the money to buy and to run it (and doing all the other things associated with it). The result was an average 'speed' (distance over time) not much faster than the average pre-industrial peasant could walk and certainly a lower figure than bus, rail or cycling calculated on the same basis. Of course, owning and driving a car can be desirable and pleasurable in itself , so the calculation is a provocative metaphor rather than a proof that driving is foolish. But it suggests that – for at least those who do not like cars in themselves – having to drive can be a 'time thief' even if on the surface it appears to be a time saver.

The hidden speed of slowness

Slow food

The 'slow food' movement (which originated as a protest against 'fast food') proposes not that it is good to have to wait longer in a burger queue, but rather that traditional approaches to cooking and eating have broader benefits – of conviviality, celebration, neighbourliness, relaxation, shared ritual, participating in and renewing cultural traditions – that more than make up for the longer time they take. It is the package that matters. We have to see the McDonalds 'offer' – ten minutes from deciding to eat to throwing a tangle of packaging into the bin, as opposed to spending an hour or more in a restaurant, or half a day preparing and sharing a truly excellent meal with friends – as only one element of a much wider transaction. The apparent time saving may in fact be a theft of time if the 'fast eaters' then have to spend more time than they have saved getting the satisfactions and benefits they have foregone in other ways. It is an impoverishment if they do not have other ways.

Slow lifestyles

This may offer a clue to the paradox we noted at the beginning of this chapter, of more and more 'time saving' seeming to come together with more and more pressure on, and shortage of, time. Contrast two caricature lifestyles. First, an extreme modern urban lifestyle, abounding in speed and time saving: driving a fast sports car between gym (for concentrated exercise), massage (for concentrated relaxation), supermarket (for time-saving ready meals), airport (for brief escape to concentrated wilderness experience), art group (for concentrated self-expression) and occasionally home (to eat ready meals in front of the television watching *Eastenders* for concentrated fix of gossip and human interaction, and to sleep briefly in order to be up in time for the gym before work) and possibly to therapist (for fast-track identification and resolution of emotional and psychosocial problems.) Second, a caricature traditional lifestyle: clanking slowly on a heavy old bicycle through a park, greeting some neighbours on the way, to an old fashioned corner shop where a long wait in the queue provides an opportunity to both give and receive sympathy and wise advice from others; home on the bicycle again to exercise ingenuity and creativity in coaxing a tasty meal out of the limited raw ingredients available at the shop.

Clearly a trek in rainforest beats a cycle ride through an English municipal park for vibrancy of wilderness experience. The same can be said for many of the other pairs of options in this comparison. But this is only part of the point. By being separated, splintered and commoditised, the activities in the first example, however individually vivid, may take longer to nourish the same range of human desires and demands than the second set. For all the speed of our modern icon's sports car as it races from one traffic light to the next on the way to the next service outlet, the overall rate of satisfaction gained may have dwindled so far that there are not enough hours in the day to glean the minimum gratification necessary for happiness and fulfilment – especially if the whole frenetic round is also having to be fitted around a job whose time demands outstrip its quality of life compensations.

However bland, dull and slow the second lifestyle may seem, most of its activities provide several benefits at once. The cycle ride provides exercise, experience of being out moving freely in fresh air and nature, and possibly some social contact. Unlike a rainforest trek, the municipal park provides its (milder) pleasures as part of the daily round, at a cost of zero pounds and zero minutes of travel time to get there, so its cost-benefit ratio betters the best possible exotic holiday bargain. The queue in the shop is also socially enriching, in a way that the queue at a supermarket, or a drive-thru burger or video outlet, rarely is. Most people's real neighbours may be less interesting than those in *Eastenders* but talking to them provides real social interaction rather than a simulacrum. Thus the quality of the experience of a cycle ride through the municipal park is more important than the straight comparison suggests. The opportunity for a high quality 'mundane' experience of a collective asset such as a park is a good whose value is hard to quantify, but whose absence would be keenly felt as a blow to one's personal well-being.[43]

The first lifestyle is also:

- Far better for economic growth (because it is packed with high value commercial transactions whose equivalents in the second lifestyle are cheap, free or untraded)
- Far more environmentally intensive (driving, flying, throwing away ready meal packaging)

■ Destructive rather than supportive of social capital (since its transactions are largely commercial, depersonalised, independent of spatial community and only weakly connected even to any community of interest)

These characteristics do not necessarily always come together. But they often do. And this comparison provides a further illustration of many themes of this paper.

The slowness of speed

We tend to take the physical maximum speed of the fastest machine involved in an activity as a proxy for the speed of the activity. Flying from Edinburgh or Brussels to London is perceived as faster than the train because it involves a machine capable of 600mph - even if this machine spends half an hour circling Heathrow at an effective speed of zero, and the time spent in airport formalities and getting to and from airports at speeds of around 20mph means that the train, averaging 100 or 130mph, gets you to your destination faster.

The same fallacy applies (but with an even higher carbon cost) to supersonic flight. Racing across the Atlantic in Concorde to a meeting in New York and back the same day was seen as the pinnacle of business decisiveness – with little speculation over whether the quality of interaction might be higher by videoconference in which neither party was fuddled by an early start, hours of noisy travel and time zone dislocation.

Possession of a fast car is seen as a sign of 'life in the fast lane' (a revealing metaphor) regardless of whether the car actually spends most of its life in stop-start traffic. There is a perversely inverse relationship between the rising average maximum speed of the UK's car stock and the dropping average speed of its traffic. (The irrelevance of physical potential in most circumstances was cheekily captured by a 1970s advertisement for the Citroen 2CV which showed a 2CV doing its maximum speed of 70mph, happily overtaking a Porsche 911 in a busier lane doing 68mph.)

Shrinking the world makes it smaller

A further twist to the issue of time is that where speed is genuine, this too can rob us of experience. The air industry's proudest boast – that it annihilates distance, brings places closer together, shrinks the world – is in fact arguably an impoverishment. A smaller world is, well, smaller. It is of little advantage either to business people who are now expected to fly across the Atlantic with as little hesitation as they would have caught the train between London and Liverpool a few decades ago, or to tourists who simply have to go further to get the same degree of remoteness, exoticism and escape. Remoteness and ease of access are in fact opposite concepts, and it is remarkable that the air travel industry has managed to prevent this fact being more widely recognised.

The same trade-off arises at more parochial scales. Travelling under one's own power - by foot or cycle - enlarges the world, and loads with significance and occasion journeys and arrivals which by car are banal and meaningless. Britain is a huge, diverse, mysterious and challenging country when traversed by bike or on foot. Sodden, bedraggled and knackered hikers and cycle tourists may look absurd and pathetic from the comfort of the cars zooming past them. But they are doing it in order to inhabit a larger, richer and more vivid world, for which the discomfort is a price worth paying.

Overshoot and optimality

It is also true that cars, planes, and wealth have brought potentially mind-broadening and enriching travel within the reach of far more people. As with many propositions in this paper, it is a question of degree: of the point at which something which, when scarce, was undoubtedly a benefit becomes first more compromised and ambiguous, and eventually causes more harm than good. Arguably we have passed this point with travel. We travel more and further, and it means less and less. What the motorised travel industry presents as gifts of experience are in fact thefts of significance.

Exercise provides another example. Mechanisation has brought most people in developed economies the great blessing of not having to do arduous and exhausting physical labour all day every day. This is unquestionably an advance. But continuing to mechanise work and transport until physical activity is so designed out of normal life than people have to make special, conscious efforts to get the minimum amount of exercise prudent for cardiovascular and muscular health is folly. A 'middle way' where enough exercise is built in to the ordinary daily routine of most people's lives to keep them healthy would be better than either extreme.

Slow lifestyles provide a different example. It was mostly women who had to ride old bicycles laboriously to restricted shops, spend time being polite to neighbours whether they liked them or not, spend hours in kitchens patiently preparing raw ingredients, and so on. Modern consumer society has been genuinely liberating. But it may now be argued that it has gone too far, and enslaved people in new circles of drudgery (much of it now revolving around cars). Social research suggests that women are still getting the raw end of the deal – expected to chauffeur children, do more than their share of housework (albeit mechanised) and do full time paid jobs to pay for all the commoditised services. But this does not justify sentimentality about aspects of past lifestyles that were tedious, limiting and discriminatory.

The lesson of all these examples is that development paths, just like consumption growth, can encounter diminishing returns and eventually negative returns. The secret of successful policy is to recognise when 'enough is enough', and change direction before overshoot begins to erode the gains made. Policy should seek the optimal balance of different aims, not pursue some of them to the utmost.

7| A better choice of choice

'Choice' is the beginning of debate, not the end

Chapter 5 suggested that simply claiming that a policy or change 'increases choice' does not prove it is good, still less that it is better than alternatives. The invocation of the notion of choice should be the start of discussion, not its end. Often choice is a good. But choices of some kinds or for some people can preclude or constrain other kinds of choices for the same people and for others. Whether the increase to some people is worth the losses to others is inescapably a matter of judgement, guided by political values grounded in moral principle. The questions of when benefits to one group justify losses to another, and what kinds of intervention to reallocated benefits are legitimate, are perennial topics of ethics. The equally perennial arguments between libertarian and egalitarian political aims, and between increasing or reducing the role of the state, are political reflections of them.

A barrier to progress is the widespread assumption that the alternative to 'consumerist' choice sets is not the 'sustainable' one, but a third kind which could be called 'hair shirt'. The transport 'hair shirt' choice set, as widely perceived, entails people being prevented from driving by punitive taxation and/or intrusive regulation, and therefore being forced to rely on public transport which is as slow, inflexible, unreliable and uncomfortable as ever but also chronically overcrowded, to reach a restricted range of choices in occupation, recreation and services. The perceived food/agriculture 'hair shirt' choice set features having to queue up in small shops, which are closed at evenings and weekends when most people prefer to shop, to pay exorbitant prices for a restricted range of muddy vegetables out of dreary Victorian novels – parsnips, cabbage, Brussels sprouts – which require endless scrubbing, chopping and removal of the off bits, and remain dull and depressing to eat even after elaborate cooking.

If these views are unfair caricatures, the green movement is partly to blame. Simplistic pro-car rhetoric has sometimes provoked equally simplistic anti-car responses. Even many committed environmentalist vegetable-lovers have given up on organic box schemes which, under the slogan of seasonality, require customers to pay a fixed price and then make what they can of whatever unpredictable assortment the growers have found it convenient to offload in a given week. Farmers markets offer a more attractive deal because they do not deny choice with quite such Gosplan high-handedness: the produce may still be (by supermarket standards) restricted, small, oddly shaped, muddy and overpriced, but at least you don't have to buy anything you don't actually want – a perfectly reasonable exercise of choice.

The need for long term policy

But a worse problem is the asymmetry in timing of any attempts to change the current choice sets. Attempts to reduce traffic (for example) do tend to create genuine and conspicuous inconvenience immediately. The benefits would come later and indirectly. A politics based on maximising immediate gratification is incapable of structural change. A more grown-up political culture, in which it is possible to argue for policies on the basis of policies five, ten or more years into the future, is a prerequisite for sustainability.

Fortunately this pendulum seems to be swinging back. Faced with the evidence of the failure of policy positions based too much on short-term consumer choice, politicians are starting to make the case for longer term approaches. Current debates about infrastructure investment and taxation to fund better public services, and about transport investment and food and agriculture reform in particular, indicate the dawn of what could be called a new realism.

Example: an anticipatory, preventive approach to public transport

In 1989 Vienna City Council built a substantial new suburb of high density flats on the outskirts of the city. Before any of them were occupied, the local shopping centre was built, including food shops and the terminus of a new tram line, with a service running every 10 minutes into the city centre from early morning to late evening. At a micro level all those empty trams were wasteful. But they achieved an important 'macro' goal of the city council: that in the creation of the new suburb there should never be a point at which any of its residents should need to use a car to get to the amenities and services they wanted. The council had the confidence to formulate such a goal – and the financial freedom and muscle to run a public service 'inefficiently' in the short term to achieve it.

A more sophisticated approach to 'evidence'

Paradoxically, the Government's commitment to 'evidence-based policy' is potentially a barrier to a longer term policies for the public good. In many fields the evidence about a decision's effects on short term and private interests is much better than that about its longer term and public interest effects. For example, many of the potential costs to businesses of the land use planning system are direct, immediate, and certain and straightforward to measure in monetary terms. Examples include the time and effort businesses need to spend applying and negotiating for planning permission; the extra costs of meeting requirements and standards that may be required as conditions for planning consent, such as infrastructure, environmental standards, and community facilities demanded as planning gain; and profits and business opportunities lost as a result of the planning process refusing, delaying or restricting development, or setting prohibitively expensive conditions.

In contrast many potential benefits of planning – convenient, healthy, attractive environments, efficient land use patterns and reliable infrastructure and services, management of risk (e.g. pollution, accidents, floods) – tend to be indirect, long term, and multi-causal, and therefore difficult to attribute to planning interventions. The benefits of risk prevention are particularly hard to quantify since, if it is successful, the costs never make an appearance.

Of course this does not prove that these benefits always result, still less that they will always exceed or justify the short term disbenefits. The point is rather that the asymmetry in evidence availability between provable, measurable, direct short term commercial benefits and speculative, indirect, intangible longer term disbenefits means that an over-literal faith in 'evidence' tends to favour the former and devalue the latter. The apparently healthy, neutral, ideology-free empiricism of the commitment to 'evidence-based policy' in fact conceals a systemic bias in favour of short term and private interests.

To overcome this we need a rather more sophisticated and sceptical view of the nature and pitfalls of 'evidence', and recognition that 'absence of evidence is not evidence of absence', and a readiness to give judgement enough weight on the many consequences of public policy for which direct objective evidence is not available.

Eco-efficiency and paths to wellbeing

The diagram oooposite summarises some assumptions and realities about different choice sets and their effects on the environment and well-being. The current mix of goods and services increases wellbeing by providing more (perceived) choice, more (perceived) convenience, etc., but at an environmental cost. The 'hair shirt' model, instead, is currently less environmentally harmful, but also less convenient, fun, varied – there is assumed to be an inverse relationship between environment and quality of life. Instead, the sustainable model we are proposing (labelled 'richer choices') is assumed to be somewhere in between: less starkly austere and eco-friendly than the hairshirt model, but not as hedonistic or as environmentally profligate as the present position. 'Richer choices' is a world in which more people substitute use of services for purchase of physical products; use energy- and material-intensive goods and services much more sparingly; have a lower turnover of consumer goods – which become seen truly as 'durables' rather than disposables - and have less waste to take for recycling and disposal; and in which more public space becomes enjoyable and usable in its own right, rather than being an arena to traverse as rapidly as possible between private spaces.

It is similar to what many people seek and relish in holidays as disparate as a stay in a remote rural cottage or gites, or a walking or cycling tour, or a continental city break. These superficially quite different experiences all have in common a simplification, a paring down of routine material clutter to clear time and attention for more vivid and intense engagement with the landscape, the weather, the cultural life of a city, and/or one's companions. Of course enjoying an interlude as peasant, wanderer or flaneur does not necessarily make these desirable models for routine life, and anyway many people also enjoy holidays that pile on extra technological elaborations or redouble their eating, drinking and shopping. But if many people find life most vivid, intense and fulfilling precisely when their customary patterns

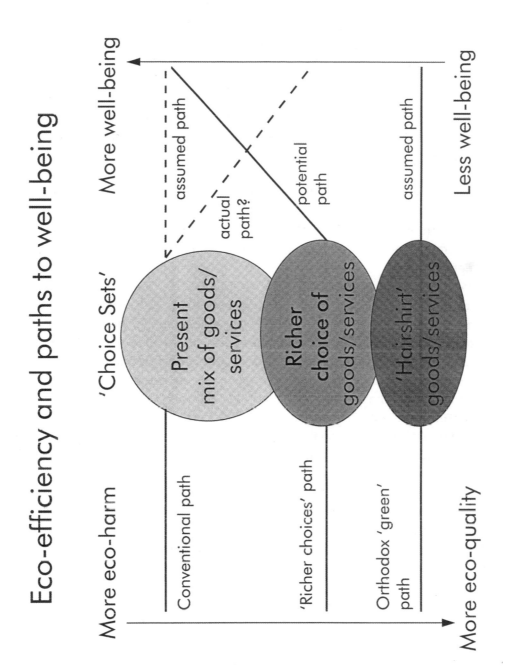

Eco-efficiency and paths to well-being

of material consumption and possession are suspended, this suggests that what counts as normal consumption can obstruct as well as fulfil life.

Over time, the current mix of goods and services is likely to lead to less well-being for instance, for most people driving is an increasingly frustrating, stop-start, niggling, unfree exercise – the opposite of the speed, daring, freedom, emancipation still promoted by advertising. Conversely the sustainable model is likely to produce more well-being. If the two lines cross, richer choices is the better long term option on social as well as environmental grounds.

What would a richer life be like?

Much of this paper criticises what is damaging about current patterns of consumption and the policies that promote them. So what is the positive alternative? Elements of it are scattered through the paper: this section brings them together.

'Developed' countries such as the UK have achieved extraordinary levels of material production, have social and economic institutions of remarkable subtlety and capacity, and open societies in which it is possible to debate matters of social value and political choice freely. With all these advantages it is dismal that we have allowed the situation to develop where large numbers of people lack even the basics of a decent and fulfilling life; that even the better off live under debilitating stress and anxiety, and that technology is applied in ways that accelerate rather than slowing environmental damage. We really ought to do much better.

However, political and social change must start from where we are, and will be muddled and piecemeal. People will always live in a range of different ways; and no political programme will magically transform human nature. So we do not offer any facile utopia. Instead we propose directions of change which we believe would be better for human wellbeing, fulfilment and security than fatalistic acceptance of current trends. The core ideas are choosing which choices matter; and treating material consumption as a means to human welfare not an end in itself.

Security before plutocracy

Insecurity and anxiety are debilitating. For most people, a richer life would be one free from financial insecurity and fear of poverty. Certainty of a retirement income adequate for a modestly decent way of life would make a major contribution. A commercial pension industry based on stock market investment has proved itself incapable of providing such security. The state pension would be restored to a 'liveable' level. The cost would be funded from universal progressive taxation. The experience of the last few years may make many people regard paying more tax for the certainty of a decent state pension as a better bargain than having to pay size-able commission to a private pension provider and take a gamble on their fund managers' acumen and the ups and downs of the stock market.

Good local public services

The vast majority of families would send their children to the nearest school, use the local library, and register with the nearest doctor, dentist and providers of any other public services they need, confident in the expectation that these will all provide a good service. The reduction in need to travel would reduce the cost of living, effectively making everyone better off and reducing the level of pension needed for decency. It would also reduce resource use and improve local environments, and the localisation of services would bolster community identity.

Quality in day to day life: investment in public space

Partly through reduced travel and car use, but also through serious investment in parks, gardens, street ambience and other public spaces, the quality of the public realm would be raised. People would get pleasure and enrichment from moving around their own neighbourhoods. The pleasures of place and character we currently head for France or Italy for - unique local cafes, atmospheric squares - will be recognised as blessings we can and should create for ourselves. And having done so, we will not need to 'escape' to special places so frequently or urgently.

Restoring the specialness of travel

Long distance travel would revert to being something occasional and special. Arguably we would then get more pleasure from it. It would certainly cause less damage.

Different ways to show off and mark status

People would compete less on brute volume of consumption – the biggest and most powerful car(s), the most foreign holidays – and more on quality or exquisiteness. Hand made furniture, craft items, adornments would be prized as signals of sophistication and status.

Richly layered lifestyles

The patterns of life sketched here would combine multiple satisfactions. Exercise, neighbourly human contact, pleasure in surroundings would be built in to day to day activity, reducing the need for people to (literally) go out of their way to obtain them.

Low energy and environmental impacts

The environmental cost – especially the 'carbon cost' – of life would be much reduced, through a combination of thorough, systematic application of well-known green technologies (insulation, combined heat and power, reuse and recycling of wastes) and lifestyle patterns (more use of local, unpackaged produce; less travel, over shorter distances, at lower speeds) which avoid the 'rebound' effects that currently negate technical improvements.

Feedback loops

The various elements of the society sketched above would tend to support each other. Good local amenities would reduce the need to travel, both improving the quality of the public realm and giving more people more time and incentive to move about locally on foot or by bike. This will further improve the public realm, increase the denseness and richness of social interactions and strengthen local communities, which will further reduce the need to travel. This will also reduce the need for cash to buy a better quality of life – which will make more palatable the public spending needed on good public services. But the reduction in need for transport infrastructure and social services to remedy problems caused by current high anxiety, high mobility, low community lifestyles will help offset the costs.

But what about growth?

A society of the kind just sketched would probably have lower GDP per capita than at present. We hope it will be clear that, apart from the technical problem of managing the transition from the current growth-driven economy to this more benign one, this would not matter.

8| Policy implications

This study did not set out either to propose new practical policies or initiatives for sustainability or to develop detailed work programmes for particular topics or sectors. Instead, its practical payoff is to help make sense of the vast amount of work of this kind which has already been done, by:

- Bringing out and clarifying some principles and assumptions that have far-ranging potential to underpin and justify practical sustainability policies and initiatives
- Showing the underlying consistency and coherence between currently unrelated sustainable policies in different fields, notably reductions in greenhouse gas emissions and advances in waste minimisation, and between transport policy and public health
- Distinguishing policies and initiatives which have potential to work towards genuine sustainability from those which merely palliate, disguise or displace unsustainability

This chapter makes a start. First it distils the thinking of the paper into a few general principles of policy making for sustainability. Second it proposes some more practical approaches to put these into effect.

A political pendulum

Over the last quarter century the 'long wave' pendulum of political values has swung to an extreme of individualism, market based solutions, and hostility to and distrust of anything that smacks of central planning and state intervention. This has happened before. But the discrediting and ignominious collapse of the planned economies of eastern Europe has left the discourse of individualism, choice and liberty so pervasive, and the image of collectivism, social choice and mutuality so tarnished, that we are in danger of forgetting that there is actually a debate to be had or a pendulum that can swing.

This matters because - as this paper argues - individualism is not increasing well-being at all reliably for the affluent; is disadvantaging the poor; and is making environmental problems politically intractable. For these reasons an important task of this project is to renew the possibility of taking collective solutions seriously. Private choices are always conditioned by the quality of the public goods and wider networks within which any consumer must operate. The use of 'choice' as short-hand for personal sovereignty and empowerment as private consumer conceals this. When this happens, what is presented as 'choice', and may even be experienced as choice locally, may in fact be a kind of coercion. In a complex society the choices other people make can be coercive just as much as the choices governments make - but without even the possibility of intelligent direction towards desirable goals. Neither market nor government has a monopoly of either choice or coercion. Nor, for that matter, of competence and efficiency - or their opposites.

Principles of policy making for sustainability

In the light of this we propose four principles.

1. Conscious decision about the purpose and direction of economic policy

Globalisation, competition, footloose investment and so on are not immutable laws of nature, but human constructs. They happen because we make them happen. The current trend towards liberalisation is not the natural and inevitable state of affairs, but a historically unusual extreme of economic interconnectedness, made possible by technology but only achieved and maintained through sustained efforts by companies and governments.

Domestically the proportion of decisions taken through market and quasi-market mechanisms is historically unprecedented. Again this has come about not through historical inevitability but by conscious and determined action, especially by the Thatcher, Major and Blair governments and their business advisers and partners.

There is little point arguing over whether we should have come this way in the first place, because we are here now. But there is no good reason why we must keep going in the same direction. (Intellectual laziness, lack of imagination or ambition, fatalism and vested interest are not good reasons!) In economic policy we should now consciously take stock of where we have got to, and decide explicitly where we want to go next.

> Government should initiate and lead an open national debate about the purpose and future direction of the economy. This should not make any presumption that the trends towards globalisation and market mechanisms promoted by policy over the last few decades are inevitable or beneficial - or the contrary.

It is widely asserted that Government and the political process no longer has either the capacity to lead such a 'serious' debate or the credibility or power to act effectively on whatever conclusions it reached. Indeed Government's loss of authority, and the public's loss of faith in politics, are frequently quoted as reasons why globalisation and marketisation are unstoppable. But the causality may work in both directions: public disenchantment with and disengagement from the political process may be at least partly a response to Government's apparent abdication of responsibility for the nature and purpose of economic activity and the consequences of the current economic trajectory for human wellbeing, justice and security in poor as well as rich countries.

It remains true that unwinding the consumer economy as we know it now would be a dauntingly difficult political project. 'Prospect theory' in economics suggests that we value losses more than gains. People will need a lot of persuading to move away from many of the choices and kinds of consumption they now have, even if persuaded of the benefits this could bring. The 'culture of contentment' – which in many ways is a culture of insecurity and defensiveness – will fight back.

2. Growth should not be an objective

Most people want an economy that meets their needs, provides wellbeing and quality of life, and gives everyone the space and the opportunity to seek fulfilment and self realisation. That is not necessarily an economy that is getting bigger. It might be staying the same size, or shrinking, but getting better.

Economic growth (as conventionally measured in per capita GDP and related indicators) tells us virtually nothing about whether the economy is achieving any of these goals. The argument in this paper has shown that rising per capita GDP is not even a good measure of whether the poorest people are better able to meet their needs, and presented many examples and reasons why pluses in economic growth may be minuses in wellbeing as well as environmental protection. Treating growth as a proxy for wellbeing is an obstacle to policies to reconcile human wellbeing with environmental limits. Some of the most important and promising policy principles for sustainability - obviating consumption, fostering local and mutual provision - will often reduce traded activity.

Government has shown appreciation of this in principle if not always in practice. As Tony Blair put it in the Government's first statement of policy on sustainable development:

'The last hundred years have seen a massive increase in the wealth of this country and the well being of its people. But focusing solely on economic growth risks ignoring the impact - both good and bad - on people and on the environment…Now…there is a growing realisation that real progress cannot be measured by money alone…But in the past, governments have seemed to forget this. Success has been measured by economic growth - GDP - alone. We have failed to see how our economy, our environment and our society are all one. And that delivering the best possible quality of life for us all means more than concentrating solely on economic growth.'

> GDP growth should no longer be an objective of government policy. Instead, policy should aim to increase quality of life benefits (making no distinction between those bestowed by traded economic activity and those not), and reduce their environmental cost.

In particular this means that the fourth of the Government's sustainable development objectives, 'high and stable levels of economic growth and employment' is inappropriate and unhelpful and should be replaced with something on the lines of 'an economy that gives everybody the opportunity to get what they need and want for a comfortable and fulfilling life'. It is notable that a recent research report by the Cabinet Office Strategy Unit similarly supports the provision of better information on the life satisfaction consequences of alternative lifestyle choices.[44]

3. Choice should be a means, not an end

Individual choice in markets or quasi-markets does not necessarily lead to the best, good or even tolerable outcomes. Individual choices have cumulatively led to an overall situation that no sane person would have chosen in transport. Parental choice is a major obstacle to providing acceptable standards for all in school education. In food and agriculture, a superabundance of trivial choice masks the absence of more important ones. The shift from state provision to market choice in financial services (especially pensions) has proved oppressive and bewildering, led to exploitation of many vulnerable people and deprived even the most prudent of security.

Increasing some choices precludes others. It is not good enough just to say that a policy 'increases choice': policy makers must consider whether the choices being increased are useful and important ones, and consider the choices thereby being precluded or prevented.

> Choice should be treated as a means to enable people to get what they want, not an end in itself. Often, the choices that really matter must be taken collectively not by individuals. Government should act to make the most valuable choice sets available.

In services including schooling and local buses, it is often choice and competition which prevent the delivery to all users of minimum acceptable standards.

Of course the two are not always or necessarily opposed. There are many cases where choice and competition can genuinely energise and drive service improvements, and others where some degree of choice is socially desirable or even morally essential. Standards may include the provision of some level of choice. Moreover, standards depend on resource levels, which are inescapably the results of choices about priorities. The point is not to eschew or oppose choice - it is simply not to put the principle of choice on a pedestal to the detriment of others.

> Standards should replace choice as the primary basis for appraising public services. Choice should not be allowed to undermine standards.

4. More government intervention

All these points lead towards the conclusion that in many areas we need more active government intervention: to move the 'choice sets' available to people towards less consumer choice but more social choice; less consumption but more quality of life benefits. This has logic; it makes policy problems soluble; it seems people are increasingly ready for it;[45] it is - and can be presented as - a positive development of progressive ideas. It is also the only plausible and politically remotely practicable approach to addressing the environmental problems set out at the beginning of the paper.

> Government should be more active, ambitious and confident to intervene to secure these public goods - such as wellbeing and environmental sustainability - that cannot be achieved by individual choice. After all, this is what government is for.

This does not necessarily mean that Government should spend more. Many of the policy directions advocated throughout this document, and specific recommendations in the rest of this chapter, should reduce the need for what are now huge palliative programmes in (for example) health care, social security, waste management and transport.

Nor does it necessarily even mean more bureaucratic interventions. In many areas of policy, bold simple changes - for example ecological taxation reform, shifting tax from 'goods' to 'bads' - could allow drastic simplification or even abolition of currently elaborate and bureaucratic control systems. It is arguable that in fields such as transport funding, good intentions combined with a pathological aversion to offending or disobliging vested interests has resulted in the worst of all worlds: regulatory and administrative systems which are intrusive and obstructive yet ineffectual.

Practical approaches

The principles just outlined call for some more concrete and 'applied' approaches. These are already illustrated in the discussion of transport and food/agriculture which runs through this paper. This section sets them out explicitly, using as examples three further policy areas: health, regeneration and energy/climate change. In all of these, there are some exciting and positive developments moving in the directions advocated, but also huge inertia and backward looking habits of thought to overcome.[46] It is hoped that these comments will help guide policy in more sustainable directions.

Clarity about objectives

It should be clear what policy is for, avoiding false proxies and mistaking means for ends. (Much of the muddle in transport policy comes from treating mobility solely as an end rather than mostly as a means to the end of access.) The overall aim of health policy should be to enable people to live healthy lives as free as possible from illness and disability. Sickness treatment services are only a means to achieve this. Likewise in regeneration, the objective should be that no neighbourhoods should be stuck in a vicious circle of neglect, deprivation and degradation, so that nobody is deprived of decent living conditions and life opportunities because of where they live. Economic, social and physical interventions should all be judged against that standard. Employment policy should aim to provide everyone with the opportunity of a fulfilling and satisfying occupation or livelihood - not necessarily a 'proper' paid job. In energy, people want to be comfortable in their homes and have their food cooked, clothes cleaned, videos played, newspapers illuminated and so on: consuming energy is only a means to these ends.

> All policy should be assessed against explicit objectives for quality of life and environmental outcomes.

The options hierarchy

Clarity about objectives paves the way for a more sophisticated approach to policy options. Presented with new or increasing problems, the reflex of practitioners in any field is usually to propose an increase in service activity - for example building more hospitals or power stations, or increasing the funding for physical regeneration.

Efficiency

The current and previous governments have already struggled to shift from this 'producer' mentality on to one concerned with efficiency - getting more result out of service activity. Examples might include treating more patients in each bed space year, replacing 35-per-cent-efficient coal power stations with 65-per-cent-efficient gas ones, targeting regeneration spend more precisely on the neighbourhoods that most need it and the projects that will make the most difference. This admirable principle has had mixed results. It has led to pressure on public service workers (especially health workers) continually expected to do more with less, distortion of policy priorities, fragmentation of effort to chase often counterproductive efficiency targets, and 'dumping' of problems on other areas. There are notorious examples of the latter such as where tight targeting of regeneration incentives merely draws businesses and investments in from neighbouring areas, displacing the deprivation rather than reducing it.

Moreover, 'efficiency' only helps improve outcomes if the inputs and outputs compared in an efficiency ratio are both good proxies for the results that really matter. This paper has argued that monetary measures are often poor proxies. This makes many of the efficiency measures commonly used irrelevant if not counter-productive. For example, reducing staff such as hospital porters and orderlies or park keepers improves the apparent cost efficiency of service delivery but reduces the quality of the public realm and puts more pressure on remaining staff. A lowest-cost approach to health service catering misses opportunities both to give many less well off people (staff and patients) a better and healthier diet, and to support sustainable food and agriculture.[47] The decision of some hospital trusts (notably

Edinburgh Royal Infirmary) to sell crumbling hospitals on valuable inner-city sites for redevelopment and move to new purpose-built hospitals at peripheral locations is financially rational but disastrous for sustainable transport, urban vitality and equity, and bad for health on any measure broader than the interventions done inside the hospital.

> Public service efficiency and performance measures should cover quality of life and environmental outcomes affected. Financial proxies for these should be used warily and sceptically.

This is not to advocate further increases in monitoring and performance appraisal. The 'audit culture' - the insistence on targets, monitoring, measuring and reporting - can reduce the ability of public services to innovate, plan for the longer term or take broader issues into consideration. Arguably public services could be improved by less performance measurement on the prevailing model rather than more. The point is that so far as performance management is necessary, it should measure the right things.

Obviation

In a cluttered, over-complex and over-consuming world, policy should give much more attention to obviation - that is, avoiding the need for activities and interventions, as distinct from designing better or more efficient ones. The waste hierarchy (reduce, reuse, recycle etc.) is an example of this approach which has widespread support. In the energy sector, designing buildings to need less energy to maintain desired conditions (for example using solar gain, high thermal mass, natural daylight and 'stack effect' ventilation to reduce the need for heating, cooling and artificial light, and avoid air conditioning) is cheaper and more sustainable than any currently-available renewable energy technology.

Obviation has applications in many other sectors as well. For instance, it should be central for health. It is a platitude that 'prevention is better than cure,' and recent moves to give more attention to preventive health care are welcome. But this needs to go much further. Lifestyle factors, notably diet, exercise and freedom from pollution, poverty and debilitating anxiety, insecurity and stress are crucial for positive health. Yet food, agriculture and transport policy are not acknowledged as central concerns of health policy. Expansion of sickness treatment services is overdue and necessary, but should not be confused with, or accepted as a substitute for, a far more systematic approach to improving and maintaining health.

The perennial controversy over major infrastructure project proposals such as airports, roads, railways, power stations, reservoirs etc, and the widespread criticism of the Government's current proposals for procedural reforms designed to make it easier for developers to push such projects through quickly, show the need for deeper reform. Such reform must ensure that alternatives, especially obviation, are considered early and thoroughly, and infrastructure projects only brought forward when alternatives have been exhausted, not (as at present) as soon as a prospective developer is confident of a profit.[48]

Policy making and appraisal in all sectors should start at the top of the following hierarchy, and only proceed to lower steps when the possibility of higher ones have been exhausted:

1   Obviation: ways to avoid or reduce the need for actions or interventions, for example by preventing problems arising, or ensuring that policies in other sectors do not create or dump problems

2   Efficiency: getting more benefit from activities or interventions - making sure that efficiency is measured and promoted in terms of genuine quality of life and environmental outcomes, and with proper attention to consequences outside the immediate area of policy concern

3   New or expanded provision as a last resort, and with the greatest possible efficiency (as understood in (2))

Preventive approaches

'Prevention is better than cure' in wider fields than health. For example, regeneration has become a huge and permanent industry of consultants, facilitators, capacity builders, vision makers, architects, designers, builders, business counsellors, investment advisers, image makers and so forth, deploying vast budgets on each regeneration area before moving to the next. There are always new places needing regeneration, because the forces which cause degeneration are allowed to continue virtually unchecked until a once-decent place has sunk sufficiently into disintegration and desperation to qualify for help. These forces include the collapse of traditional industries (often due to global competition), decay of the public realm due to underinvestment and uncontrolled traffic, feedback loops of middle-class and investment flight worsening conditions for those left, encouraging more flight, collapse of community cohesiveness and social capital. It would be better, and in the long run cheaper, to pursue policies which do not cause degeneration in the first place. Some key ones would be to safeguard and increase local economic diversity, self-reliance, closure and resilience, reduce the extent to which settlements have to compete against each other for footloose trade and investment, and increase rather than decrease the costs of road transport.

Road safety provides another example. As pointed out in Chapter 5, making roads 'safer' by removing hazards such as sharp bends and blind junctions encourages traffic to go at higher speeds, at which previously safe bends and junctions in turn become 'dangerous', and candidates for further 'safety improvements'. Over a few decades a picturesque and idiosyncratic road embedded in a landscape, with bends which unwary motorists occasionally slithered off at 30mph, is turned into a characterless gash across the landscape subject to fatal 80mph accidents. As with regeneration, the industry of road 'safety improvement' is self perpetuating.

'Traffic calming' at least recognises the problem. But ironically it often takes the form of laborious and expensive retrofitting of artificial and intrusive artefacts to neutralise the effects of earlier engineering interventions that increased speeds, accompanied by a thicket of warning signs which perpetuate the idea that measures to slow traffic are freakish and exceptional, requiring notice and apology. As with regeneration, there is a simpler and cheaper preventive alternative: simply refrain from removing the speed-restraining features which un-'improved' roads have naturally, and put responsibility back on motorists to be ready for them rather than on highway authorities to signpost every hazard. This is, in essence, what 'home zones' are all about. Designing roads to be useable only at lower speeds would also have important collateral benefits of reducing fuel use, noise and signage clutter.

In all these cases, a truly preventive approach should reduce the need for public spending.

The choice not to choose; and the freedom to choose genuine alternatives

The 'choice not to choose' should be respected and provided for. For example:

- Those who have declined to take out 'stakeholder' pensions because they do not wish to gamble their pension on the stock market in even a highly regulated and safeguarded way, do not want to pay even a small proportion of their investment as fees to commercial fund managers, and do not want to have to judge the competing claims of even a small number of companies, should be able to opt to invest in an unfunded state pension guaranteeing a reasonable return linked to prices;

- Employment / economic development policy should acknowledge that many people value security above opportunity. There should be 'jobs for life' for those who want them and are willing to accept lower pay, prospects and prestige in return. Restoring a whole stratum of relatively undemanding but honourable jobs keeping the public realm safe, decent and attractive - park keepers, hospital orderlies, bus conductors, station porters, railway linesmen - brutally stripped out in the 1980s in the name of 'efficiency' - would be a good start; People should be free to choose not to be 'entrepreneurial' if they temperamentally don't like risk;

- People should be free to choose to live in local communities with higher levels of taxation, regulation and public service provision if they wish. Local authorities should have the powers to provide and impose more, subject to local election mandate. (Restrictions of local government powers and taxation in the name of 'freedom' paradoxically deprive us of this choice!) Government should encourage experiments with social democratic models of sustainable communities (such as Vauban in Freiburg) and not only speculative developer/commoditised versions such as the Greenwich Millennium Village.

Conclusion: a systemic approach

It is a commonplace (but true) that policy in different sectors need to be 'joined up' more. The examples in this paper have given a glimpse of how current policies in transport, energy, regeneration, health and food/agriculture all too often thwart and create problems for each other, while sustainable alternatives could be mutually supportive. This should not come as any surprise. Policies based on responding to private choices in separate sectors, or which take as proxy for quality of life economic measures which often reduce it, can only be expected to support each other occasionally by lucky accident.

In contrast, policies all guided by and tested against the same coherent set of quality of life and environmental outcomes may be expected to support each other most of the time. This is the true role and vocation for sustainable development: not just to provide a meritorious marginal decoration for 'serious' economic policy, but to provide a unifying and directing framework for all policy.

Government should stop treating sustainable development as a distinct policy topic, separate from 'mainstream' policy domains, and recognise it instead as a coherent world view capable of unifying, reconciling and setting a consistent direction for all other policies.

References

1   This tension between aspiration and constraint is at the core of the two internationally accepted 'classic' definitions: the 'Brundtland' definition that 'sustainable development is development that meets the needs of the present without compromising the ability of future generations to meet their own needs', *Our Common Future*, World Commission on Environment and Development, 1987, and the 'Caring for the Earth' definition that 'improving the quality of life within the carrying capacity of supporting ecosystems', *Caring for the Earth,* International Union for the Conservation of Nature, 1991. Sustainable development requires reconciling these, not merely balancing or trading them off.

2   Of course, all things never are equal. The mix of goods and services consumed changes as the amount increases. This can alter the environmental intensity of the consumption for better or worse, and the conditions under which this is good or bad are an important issue for eco-efficiency arguments. But the default assumption – what can be expected to happen unless some other factor changes it – must be that growth will tend to raise environmental consumption.

3   Again, all things never are equal. The relationship between innovation, environmental loading and profit is much more complex than this, as we will discuss later. But again there is clearly a default expectation that resource productivity will improve over time.

4   This whole section draws on the Government's own data and analysis in the national sustainable development indicators set, *Quality of Life Counts*, DETR, 1999, and its 2001 and 2002 updates, which provide clear information for the UK for 1970 to 2000.

5   *Economic Growth and Environmental Sustainability*, P Ekins, Routledge, 2000

6   *Living on Thin Air: The New Economy*, C Leadbeater, Penguin, 2000

7   Or 'digital' or 'weightless' or 'knowledge' economy: the terms are used overlappingly and definitions are fluid so it can be difficult to pin down exactly what its proponents are claiming, but the core idea is that computing and telecommunications technologies are making the creation and transmission of knowledge and information more important in economic life than the production and consumption of physical goods.

8   *Digital Futures: Living in a dot-com world*, J Wilsdon, Earthscan and Forum for the Future, 2001

9   *Green Political Thought*, A Dobson, Routledge, 1995; 'Human needs and wants' by M Douglas, D Gasper, S Ney and M. Thompson in *Human Choice and Climate Change, Volume 1: The Societal Framework*, S Rayner and E L Malone, Batelle Press, 1998; *Consuming People: From political economy to theatres of consumption*, A F Firat and N Dholakia, Routledge 1998

A Better Choice of Choice

10   *Consumption*, R Bocock, Routledge, 1993

11   *Greening the North: A post-industrial blueprint for ecology and equity*, W Sachs, M Linz et al, Zed Books, 1998

12   In this it is actually no different to GDP used as a measure of wellbeing since this is only valid to the extent that the traded price of goods and services reflects their contribution to wellbeing. Indeed this is arguably more arbitrary than ISEW since the latter at least tries, however inadequately, to correct for the some of the most obvious ways that market price fails to reflect wellbeing.

13   *The Joyless Economy*, T Scitovsky, OUP, 1976 and *Social Limits to Growth*, F Hirsch, Routledge, 1977.

14   'Town and country life' by N Stratford and I Christie in *British Social Attitudes: the 17th report*, Sage, 2000.

15   'It's more than money' by R Worcester in *The Good Life*, I Christie and L Nash (eds), Demos, 1998

16   *Life Satisfaction: The State of Knowledge and Implications for Government*, N Donovan and D Halpern, Cabinet Office Strategy Unit, 2002; *Does Money Buy Happiness? A Longitudinal Study Using Data on Windfalls*, J Gardner and A Oswald, Warwick University, 2001

17   *The Overworked American*, J Schor, Basic Books, 1992; and *The Overspent American*, J Schor, Basic Books, 1998

18   *Britain's World of Work – myths and realities*, R Taylor, ESRC, 2002.

19   *Britain on the Couch*, O James, Arrow, 1998.

20   *Unhealthy Societies*, R Wilkinson, Routledge, 1996; *Consumption*, R Bocock, Routledge, 1993; 'Economics, Ethics and Green Consumerism' by J Paavola in *Exploring Sustainable Consumption*, M J Cohen and J Murphy, Pergamon, 2001

21   T*he Quality of Life*, M Nussbaum and A Sen (eds), OUP 1993

22   'From Production to Consumption: Environmental policy in the European Union' by J Murphy and 'Economics, Ethics and Green Consumerism' by J Paavola in *Exploring Sustainable Consumption*, M J Cohen and J Murphy, Pergamon, 2001; 'Noticing inconspicuous consumption' by E Shove and A Warde from the Reader distributed for the Consumption, Everyday Life and Sustainability Summer School, Lancaster University, 1999

23   *Real-Life Economics*, Paul Ekins and Manfred Max-Neef (eds), Routledge, 1992

24   Personal communication

25   'Household Consumption, Quality of Life, and Environmental Impacts: A Psychological Perspective and Empirical Study' by B Gatersleben and C Vlek in *Green Households? Domestic consumers, environment and sustainability*, K J Noorman and T S Uiterkamp (eds) Earthscan, 1998

26 'Income and Happiness: Towards a Unified Theory', *The Economic Journal*, July 2001

27 *Satisfaction and Comparison Income*, A E Clark and A J Oswald, LSE 1995

28 It has two other intriguing implications. First, the proportion of people who can regard themselves as successful in life will stay exactly the same regardless of how wealthy a society is. Second, even the rich can only know they have 'succeeded' in life when they know they are about to die. This apparently happily cynical view of life thus turns out surprisingly bleak and pessimistic on examination.

29 'Noticing inconspicuous consumption' by E Shove and A Warde from the Reader distributed for the Consumption, Everyday Life and Sustainability Summer School, Lancaster University, 1999

30 'Quality of Life' by M Jacobs from the Reader distributed for the Consumption, Everyday Life and Sustainability Summer School, Lancaster University, 1999

31 This is why more sophisticated measures of economic welfare such as ISEW generally reflect some measure of inequality.

32 'Economics, Ethics and Green Consumerism' by J Paavola in *Exploring Sustainable Consumption*, M J Cohen and J Murphy, Pergamon, 2001

33 *The Cunning of Unreason: making sense of politics*, J Dunn, Harper Collins 2001

34 *Transport and Accessibility: The perspectives of disadvantaged communities*, K Lucas and R Simpson, report for the Joseph Rowntree Foundation, Transport Studies Unit, University of Westminster, 2000

35 *Commodities and Capabilities*, A Sen, Elsevier 1985.

36 *Exploring Sustainable Consumption*, M J Cohen and J Murphy, Pergamon, 2001

37 *The Green Consumer Guide*, J Elkington and J Hailes, Victor Gollancz, 1989; *Green Political Thought*, A Dobson, Routledge 1995; *Seeing Green*, J Porritt, Blackwell, 1984

38 And are influenced by their 'capabilities' in Sen's terminology.

39 *Consumerism as a Way of Life*, S Miles, Sage 1998

40 This section draws on Henley Centre research.

41 For example in 2001 Abbey National deliberately worsened the interest rates on some postal accounts which had initially offered high interest rates in return for high minimum sums invested and restrictions on withdrawal. They avoided publishing the information in any way which would have alerted customers to the fact that the accounts were now paying well below the rates on other accounts, including newer Abbey National ones without the restrictions. Thousands of investors who assumed that a household name like Abbey National would maintain the 'deal' these accounts offered (if not the absolute interest rate), and who had not troubled to review and compare all interest rates frequently, lost out.

42 *Greening the North: A post-industrial blueprint for ecology and equity*, W Sachs, R Loske, M Linz et al, Zed Books, 1998

43   This is a key motivation of the Quality of Life Capital assessment methodology which seeks to recognise and manage the value of the everyday as well as the special. See www.qualityoflifecapital.org.uk

44   *Life Satisfaction: The State of Knowledge and Implications for Government*, N Donovan and D Halpern, Cabinet Office Strategy Unit, 2002

45   For example, the remarkably easy acceptance of London's congestion charging suggests dawning recognition that restricting individual freedoms may be justified by collective benefits.

46   *State of Sustainable Development in the UK: central/local government focus*, R Levett and R Therivel, Sustainable Development Commission, 2001.

47   *Food Procurement for Health and Sustainable Development*, Sustainable Development Commission 2002